THE SUCCESS PYRAMID

THE SUCCESS PYRAMID

A SCIENTIFIC FORMULA FOR GETTING EVERYTHING YOU DESIRE

DONALD W. CAUDILL, PHD

© Copyright 2025– Donald W. Caudill

All rights reserved. This book is protected by the copyright laws of the United States of America. No part of this publication may be reproduced, stored in or introduced into a retrieval system, or transmitted, in any form or by any means (electronic, mechanical, photocopying, recording or otherwise), without the prior written permission of the publisher. For permissions requests, contact the publisher, addressed "Attention: Permissions Coordinator," at the address below.

Published and distributed by:

SOUND WISDOM
P.O. Box 310
Shippensburg, PA 17257-0310
717-530-2122

info@soundwisdom.com

www.soundwisdom.com

While efforts have been made to verify information contained in this publication, neither the author nor the publisher assumes any responsibility for errors, inaccuracies, or omissions. While this publication is chock-full of useful, practical information; it is not intended to be legal or accounting advice. All readers are advised to seek competent lawyers and accountants to follow laws and regulations that may apply to specific situations. The reader of this publication assumes responsibility for the use of the information. The author and publisher assume no responsibility or liability whatsoever on the behalf of the reader of this publication.

The scanning, uploading and distribution of this publication via the Internet or via any other means without the permission of the publisher is illegal and punishable by law. Please purchase only authorized editions and do not participate in or encourage piracy of copyrightable materials.

ISBN 13 TP: 978-1-64095-519-6

ISBN 13 eBook: 978-1-64095-520-2

For Worldwide Distribution, Printed in the U.S.A.

1 2 3 4 5 6 7 8 / 29 28 27 26 25

In memory of

My father,
Alfred Caudill

My brother,
Steven P. Caudill

My paternal grandparents,
Francis Tilford & Vesta LaRue Caudill

My maternal grandparents,
William Gordon & Edith Robinette Wampler

and

In honor of

My mother,
Shirley Wampler Caudill

My sister,
Sherry Caudill Cooke

and

In memory or honor of numerous friends
and family members and the millions of
people who have suffered from cancer

ACKNOWLEDGMENTS

This book took over 50 years to research and write, including nearly five years that was pretty much full time. There were hundreds of people including other success researchers, colleagues, family, friends and even strangers who helped me complete this task. Mentioning everyone would be impossible. However, I would like to express my love and gratitude to the following:

To the reader, thank you so much for taking the time to study these findings and apply them to your own lives.

To the authors of the many success books and articles that I have had the pleasure of reading over the past 50 plus years. Without learning the valuable information contained in those writings, this book would not have been possible. I'm especially indebted to Don Green, Executive Director of the Napoleon Hill Foundation for giving me books, mentoring me, having numerous lunch meetings with me in which he gave me great advice and encouragement. I'm so grateful for this wonderful long friendship.

To John Martin, Publisher at Sound Wisdom, for his assistance, guidance and belief in my scientific approach to the study of success and to David Wildasin for introducing me to John.

To Dr. Jennifer Janechek and Angela Rickabaugh Shears, my editors at Sound Wisdom, for their great editing skills, suggestions for improvement and making the book more reader friendly.

To Amanda Wood Williams who worked long hours creating the book's website— https://thesuccesspyramid.com/.

To the thousands of undergraduate, MBA and doctoral students that I taught during the past 40-plus years at Morehead State University, Virginia Tech, University of Memphis, University of Tennessee at Martin, University of North Alabama, Southern Arkansas University, Bluefield State University, Belmont University, Bluefield University (BU) and Gardner-Webb University (GWU). Though impossible to name specific students without missing many, I do want to acknowledge the six students from my Fall 2020 *Science of Success* Honors course at GWU—Sydney Burroughs, Sarah Morrow, Stephen Qualls, Emma L. Rayfield, Nicole Riha, and Rebekah Vaughn, my former MBA students Jon & Heather Bridges Moore, and Dr. Philip J. Slater, one of my former doctoral students with whom I have written numerous journal articles. Moreover, I am grateful for the assistance of my GWU colleagues (in alphabetical order by first name)—Dr. Angie Smith, Dr. Anna Hamrick, Dr. Anthony Negbenebor, Dr. Arielle McKee, Ashley Chapman, Dr. Ben Leslie, Dr. Bobbie Cox, Dr. Carmen Butler, Dr. Crystal Brown, Dr. Dale Lamb, Dr. David Campbell, Dr. David Carscaddon, Dr. Earl Godfrey, Dr. Ellen Sousa, Dr. Erin Cook, Dr. Felice Policastro, Frances Sizemore, Chuck and Dr. Franki Burch, Prof. Ghassan Dib, Dr. Helen S. Tichenor, Dr.

James Morgan, Dr. Jason Willis, Prof. Jay Zimmer, Dr. Jeff Tubbs, Prof. Jessica Herndon, Jessika Raduly, Julie Runyans, Dr. June Hobbs, Karen (and Max) Davis, Dr. Kent Blevins, Dr. Lily Xiao, Dr. Lisa Luedeman, Dr. Mark Reiber, Dr. Mickey McCalf, Dr. Mischia Taylor, Dr. Nancy Bottoms, Pam Scruggs, Dr. Patricia Sparti, Prof. Rebecca Haney, Dr. Robert Bass, Dr. Sandy van der Poel, Dr. Scott Shauf, Dr. Sharon Webb, Dr. Shea Stuart, Dr. Sophia Steibel, Dr. Stefka Eddins, Prof. Susan Manahan, Stephen Sain, Teresa Davis, Dr. Thomas H. Jones, Dr. Tim Zehnder, Dr. Tony Eastman, Dr. Tracy Jessup, Dr. Van Graham and many others. Finally, I thank GWU for the sabbatical during the 2021—2022 academic year and Kevin Bridges, the Interlibrary Loan Coordinator at GWU, who chased down numerous "out of print" and very expensive "success" books.

To all my professors at Berea College (especially the late Dr. Dorothy Brown and Dr. John J. Crowden), Morehead State University, University of Memphis, and Virginia Tech. I am especially grateful to my doctoral marketing professors at Virginia Tech who instilled in me a burning desire to examine issues scientifically. Many of them are now deceased—Paul F. Anderson (Advanced Marketing Research), James E. "Jim" Littlefield (International Marketing), John Thomas "Tom" Mentzer (Channels of Distribution), A. Coskun "Josh" Samli (Retailing), Robert L. "Bob" King (Advertising/Promotion), and Jeffrey E. "Jeff" Danes (Multivariate Data Analysis in Marketing). Those still living include Kent Monroe (Pricing), Edward F. "Ed" Fern (Product/Brand Management), M. Joseph "Joe" Sirgy (Consumer Behavior), Stephen W. "Steve" Clopton (Industrial/B2B Marketing), and others.

To the many people who provided much-needed prayer and substance during my battle with cancer and while I was bringing this book to completion including my former graduate student, Rev. Dr. Joanne Jacene DeVoe, who died at age 60 of a heart attack on January 8, 2025, and her husband, Butch, my former colleague at BU, Mary (Ruth) Blankenship, who died at age 51 of breast cancer on September 9, 2024, and her husband, John, Fredrick L. McQueen, fellow 1980 Berea College graduate, whose sister died of cancer on April 3, 2024, and his wife Peggy, Dr. Sue Camp, retired GWU Professor of Business whose husband Charles died of cancer on March 13, 2024, Priscilla Brooks Walker whose husband Richard died of lung cancer on June 17, 2019, Dr. Jack Weller whose wife Barbara died of esophageal cancer on March 30, 2023, Prof. Inell Knight who died of liver cancer in 1991, my aunt Cathy Wampler Sturgill who died of colon cancer, my uncle Johnny Wampler who died of leukemia in 2004, Dr. Clarence D. White who died of cancer in 2010, Dr. Gayle B. Price who died of ovarian cancer in 2012, Dr. Ann Atherton Hertzler who died of cancer in 2014, Woody Fish and his wife Pam who is battling cancer, Cathy Payne of BU and her husband John who is battling cancer, Tina Earls, who may have defeated cancer, and others.

To Bobby & Mary Ann Cassell who sent letters, texts, cards, CDs, numerous books, and Old Fashioned Lemon Drops for the sickness I had as a result of chemo therapy, and to the following friends for a plethora of assistance: George and Libbie Shipley, Tina Parker, Chad and Lisa Berry, Dr. Cheryl L. Nixon, Dr. Nancy Sowers, Dr. James Stepp, Dr. David Olive, Bethany Justis, Sherelle Morgan, Dr. Steve Peterson, Dr. Cynthis

Bascom, Dr. Crystal White Kieloch, Dr. Angela Cline, Jane B. Stephenson, Dr. Donna Henry, Marcia A. Gilliam, Valerie S. Lawson, Shannon Blevins, Dr. Sanders "Sandy" Huguenin, Paul Brammer, Dr. Irene Leech, Dr. Cedric Stone, Dr. Robert P. Lambert, Dr. Joe Alexander, Dr. Elaine Scott, Jack and Nancy Henson, Dr. Randy Wells, Randy Roberts, Larry Bledsoe, Bill Statzer, Tony Lawson, Dr. Elizabeth DeMerchant, Charles and Judy Eslinger, Tina Lewis, Lucas Beatty, Tim Havens, Casey Young, Rhonda Stidham, Donna Wilson, Dr. Daniel C. Coleman, Coach Dewey and Mily Dover Lusk, Bill and Jan Thompson, Dr. Tom and Sid Renfro, Dr. Gary and Jean Young, Scott, Stephanie, Sabryna and Sydney Cameron, Travis, Ava, Landon and Esmee Cooke, Glenn, Tyler, Sutton and Hallie Cooke, Dr. Lanna Monday, Mary Thompson, Dr. Tyler Walt, and Tim Lane.

To the memory of my friends Thomas G. Hyde, Dr. Darryl E. Gurley, Dr. Ramon P. Heimerl, Dr. Anna Burford, Dr. Max R. Carrington, Howard Feiertag, Dr. E. Thomas Garman, Dr. William E. Warren, Dr. Gil Blackburn, and Dr. Glenn Bottoms.

CONTENTS

Foreword by Don Green 15

Introduction Why It Is Important to Study "Success"
Scientifically 17

Chapter 1 I Know It When I See It 33
*Determining, Defining, and Developing
"Success Science" for You*

Chapter 2 The Blind Men and the Elephant 57
A Brief Review of Incomplete Success Theories

Chapter 3 Some Days You Eat Salads.................92
*Life Balance Theory Importance and
Why It Alone Isn't Enough*

Chapter 4 It's All About the Traits, Man............. 118
*Trait Theory Importance and
Why It Alone Isn't Enough*

Chapter 5 "It's Always Darkest Before the Dawn" 152
*New Formula, an Amazing
Discovery, and Why It Works!*

Chapter 6   What's Love Got to Do with It? 191
              Love/Gratitude, the Most Important
              Trait Hidden in Plain Sight—
              and Other Success Variables

Conclusion   Overnight Success Sometimes
              Takes a Long Time 225
              So When You Get There, Be
              Sure It's Authentic to You

Appendix A   Definitions of Success..................... 231

Appendix B   Success Rules, Keys,
              Elements found Online 239

Appendix C   Number of Components in the Various Life
              Balance Models/Theories 244

Appendix D   Hill, McCoy, St. John's Meta-Analysis 247

About Donald W. Caudill, PhD 251

FOREWORD

by Don Green

The number of new books that are published in the United States annually is about three million. It is estimated that five hundred thousand to one million of those books are based on success topics. Some success books stand out from all the rest and the same is true for Dr. Donald W. Caudill's book, *The Success Pyramid: A Scientific Formula for Getting Everything You Desire.*

In his new book, Dr. Caudill recalls his journey from humble beginnings to success as a professor, entrepreneur, and investor. He has spent his life studying Napoleon Hill and success, but more than other authors, he has applied those principles to become a remarkable success. He truly put what he learned into practice. Although Dr. Caudill has achieved a remarkable level of success, he is always reminded of his humble beginning and uses his resources to help others. He is a generous philanthropist who has donated more than a million dollars to various causes all over the country.

I urge you to read and study this book and apply what you learn to your own life. You can really have what you desire, and this book will help you to get it!

Don Green
Executive Director, Napoleon Hill Foundation
Author of several books including *Everything I Know About Success I Learned from Napoleon Hill: Essential Lessons for Using the Power of Positive Thinking*

INTRODUCTION

WHY IT IS IMPORTANT TO STUDY "SUCCESS" SCIENTIFICALLY

When I was about 12 or 13 years old, I was told nearly every day by a family member, "You're nothing. You're never going to be a somebody." You may have been told something similar, but I hope you didn't internalize this negativity. I did, until I stumbled across a paperback copy of the 1937 classic *Think and Grow Rich* by Napoleon Hill at a used bookstore. I read in this book the words "Whatever the mind can conceive and believe it can achieve," and I began to believe that if I followed Hill's principles of success, I could become a "somebody." And like many people, I achieved some success.

But during the next five or six years, I discovered that numerous people who faithfully followed Hill's principles didn't become successful. Therefore, something had to be missing, and I became determined to find out what.

Most people want a realistic formula to follow. If someone had discovered the "real" formula for success, there wouldn't be over seven billion "hits" (as of December 2024) when you type the word "success" into a search engine! Likewise, there would not be more than 3.7 billion "hits" when you limit the search to "personal success" or 278 million when you limit the search to "authentic success."

It is obvious that despite all the success manuals out there, many people are still searching for a roadmap for success. And yet, most of the advice you'll find online is inadequate, erroneous, or superfluous. What is still needed is a scientific formula for "authentic" or true success—the type of success that provides the contentment that only a life well lived can give.

SUCCESS—AN UNWIELDLY CONSTRUCT

Have you wondered why success research has not received significant scientific attention? After writing this book, I think I know. Success is an unwieldly construct—extremely difficult to define and operationalize, empirically research, and determine causality or even correlations. Now, I believe even more (to paraphrase what Winston Churchill said about Russia) that success is "a riddle wrapped in a mystery inside an enigma." Nevertheless, there have been a few major discoveries about the "science of success" in recent years. By integrating these new research findings with hundreds of years of historical data and insights, I have created a new success theory or formula that reveals how to *really* achieve sustainable, authentic, and lasting success! It should be noted that my formula will work to achieve any desire including great wealth, material possessions, power, or fame—none of which are directly correlated with authentic success.

Oscar Wilde is credited with writing, "In this world there are only two tragedies. One is not getting what one wants, and the other is getting it." Wilde notes the paradox that often when you achieve what you had deemed to be "success," it ends up not satisfying you. The most important thing is not to focus on what you want, but rather to want what you get.

Authentic success is based on your values and the pursuit of passion, purpose, or calling. This came home to me in a dramatic way in early December 2022. I had had a slight problem with swallowing food and my gastroenterologist set up an appointment for an endoscopy and the "stretching of my esophagus." During the procedure, the surgeon found that I had Stage 3 esophageal cancer.

There are only about 13,000 to 20,000 cases of esophageal cancer a year in the US, and it is deadly. One study showed it as the fourth deadliest out of about 50 cancer types, on par with pancreatic cancer. Since I was researching and writing about success, I wondered if the same principles could be applied to defeating this cancer, which has only about a 15 percent five-year survival rate—most die within two years, even with treatment. So, I took action and traveled in January 2023 at my own expense to MD Anderson in Houston, Texas, for a second opinion. MD Anderson is known as the world's leader for some cancers, including esophageal. Unfortunately, MD Anderson confirmed the diagnosis that I had received from the Levine Cancer Institute in Charlotte, North Carolina: up to one year to live with no treatment and up to two years with treatment.

The treatment plan was (1) six weeks of combined chemo-radiation therapy to shrink the tumor, and (2) an esophagectomy, which involved removing part of the esophagus and stomach and re-attaching. If there was residual cancer in the lymph nodes, then immunotherapy once a month for a year would follow. The chemo-radiation was awful. After one week, I thought I was dying. But I made it through by relying on some of the "success" techniques I was studying and much prayer.

The radial surgery went well, but four of the 23 nodes removed were cancerous and I had to start immunotherapy. At the same time, my pancreas stopped producing enzymes to digest food. During the next several months, I lost over 100 pounds. Note: I weighed 290 pounds at diagnosis and was back up to 260 for the surgery, though I had lost 30 pounds within a month of the diagnosis and 33 pounds during chemo-radiation therapy. Several weeks after surgery and days after the first immune therapy treatment, I developed double pneumonia, followed by life-threatening inflammation in both lungs. Having cancer changed my viewpoint toward what success entailed. I had originally envisioned success as getting rich and/or becoming famous. But now I was thinking more about leaving a legacy.

MYRIAD THEORIES

Like many people, I have read and studied several hundred success books. Most authors argued that people who became successful either established a balanced life (mostly across four areas) or exhibited specific traits or behaviors, had explicit goals, took definite actions, and persisted. Others maintained that becoming successful was a choice, the result of previous success(es) and/or failure(s), luck, genetics, intention, a game of giving and receiving or some nebulous quality like the law of attraction, positive thinking, or having psychic ability. In Chapter 2, I discuss each of these theories or philosophies and many others to learn how a person may achieve true, authentic, sustainable success.

Some researchers conducted actual interviews with successful people and sometimes failures and utilized frequency distributions—the least robust of all statistical analyses—to determine "traits" (i.e., talents, skills, abilities, capabilities, competences, strengths, assets, behaviors, qualities, resources, gifts—it's all semantics) that are most associated with success. However, these researchers didn't always agree which traits—I call them *resources*—were most important, even when using similar methodologies. In Chapter 4, I perform a meta-analysis of several of these studies and arrive at an astounding conclusion.

In 1937 (yes, during the Great Depression), Napoleon Hill and his third wife, Rosa Lee, created something special in *Think and Grow Rich*. Hill was one of the first authors to utilize a quasi-scientific approach to answering the question, "What causes a person to become successful?" Hill created a philosophy or theory of success by integrating (he called it "organizing") the thinking and writings of many people. In addition to organizing the existing literature (which apparently hadn't been done before), Hill maintained that he interviewed more than 500 successful people and thousands of failures over 20 years, from 1908 to 1928.

While obviously much hard work by both Hill and his wife was involved in producing the 1937 manuscript, the book was mostly another but better version of Hill's *Magic Ladder to Success* (16 principles, with the "Mastermind" newly added as a principle) published in 1930, which itself was a condensed version of his *Law of Success* (15 principles) book published in 1928. Nine of the 13 principles from *Think and Grow Rich* were essentially the same as in *Magic Ladder to Success*, with some renamed and the order of some rearranged.

However, a few principles in *Think and Grow Rich* were new or a complete reworking of principles from Hill's previous books (i.e., "sexuality: charisma and creativity," "specialized knowledge" and "decision"). In Chapter 4, I compare Hill's principles or traits in his various books to show how his thinking evolved over the years.

Hill's legacy is being masterfully managed by the Napoleon Hill Foundation on the campus of the University of Virginia's College at Wise. See their excellent website at www.naphill. org. Hill and I have a lot in common. We were both born into poverty in the same county in Virginia, though 70 years apart. Hill attended elementary school in the same building as I did. Hill and his family attended the same church as my grandfather, and his parents are buried near some of my relatives in a cemetery a mile from where I was raised.

Additionally, Hill is buried in South Carolina a few miles from where I most recently worked. Finally, Hill's son and I attended Berea College in Kentucky. Even though Hill's work is considered empirically flawed, I still have an unfathomable amount of respect for what Hill accomplished throughout his life. Only a few success writers made an equal contribution to this field of study as did Hill.

According to James Chapman, *Think and Grow Rich* ranks ninth with 30 million copies sold on his list of the most read books in the past 50 years. The *Bible* is first, followed by *Quotations from Chairman Mao*. James Clear, who deleted religious and political books because the "true" numbers *sold* can't be calculated, as millions have been given away, ranked *Think and Grow Rich* at number 12, with 70 million copies sold.

However, my dear friend Don Green,[1] Executive Director of the Napoleon Hill Foundation, says that more than 100 million copies of the book *Think and Grow Rich* have been sold. Indeed, one of the paperback copies I purchased quite a few years ago—published by Ballantine Books—has sold over 11 million copies of that version since 1987. Therefore, Hill's success principles or traits are clearly still being practiced today, and any new theory should include those that have been empirically validated.

While I had some success applying the principles in *Think and Grow Rich* as a teenager, in college, and in my career, several researchers argue that only a fraction of people—some researchers say less than 5 percent—who faithfully embrace the principles succeed. However, if the number of copies of *Think and Grow Rich* sold is *just* 50 million, then 5 percent of that would be 2.5 million—still a huge number of people becoming successful! And indeed, it has been argued that

---

1. Personal communications June 2020; August 2021; October 2021; November 2021; December 2021; February 2022, May 2024, June 2024, March 2025.

Napoleon Hill has created more millionaires than any other person in history. But research shows that "true" success is *not* equivalent to or even related to wealth creation. Becoming rich is merely a by-product of achieving authentic success.

Years ago, I realized that Hill's philosophy or theory was not organized into a framework or model that could be easily empirically or scientifically tested. And because many of the readers of Hill's book who genuinely attempted his principles did *not* become successful, I reasoned in 1976 that there had to be something or, more likely, some *things* missing in Hill's philosophy. It would have been great to talk with Hill, but in 1976 he had been deceased for about six years.

As an 18-year-old freshman at Berea College in Berea, Kentucky, in 1976, I accidentally created a theory/model not from reading Hill's or any other author's success/self-help book, but by reading numerous biographies and autobiographies— maybe as many as 100 books—about successful people. The books I read included biographies/autobiographies of historical figures, world leaders, business leaders, inventors, professional athletes, writers, musicians, actors, and celebrities. But I recently discovered that my simple theory of success, like Hill's philosophy, was not empirically testable either.

Like researchers before and after me, I was unable to find any demographics or people characteristics that were highly correlated with success. I did find that there was a slight advantage to having a high IQ, being physically attractive, and having an abundance of money and/or time—concentrated-resources theory—because they could purchase things that enhanced their ability to become successful.

My qualitative research and all the other scientists' work I consulted revealed that some successful people were born rich, but many others were born poor, some achieved success when young, some middle aged, and others when old (Albert-László Barabási, in his 2018 book *The Formula: The Universal Laws of Success* found that "age doesn't seem to matter—it's persistence!" and "success can come at any age"), some were highly educated, many were self-educated, about the same number were male and female, some were Caucasian and Christian while others were of different races and religions, some were physically attractive, but many were not, etc.

FOUR INTERTWINED SCIENCES

While successful people are demographically diverse, my eureka or aha! moment came when I discovered a *balance* of four common attributes in every successful person I had read about. Each successful person had intertwined four sciences— physiology (body), psychology (mind), sociology (heart), and philosophy (soul) in a balanced, synergistic, and harmonious way! However, I found out later that I wasn't the first person to discover this relationship—see Chapters 3 and 4. Shortly thereafter, I realized that something was still missing in my original theory if an empirically testable formula for success was to be developed. But I still had no idea what was missing! By using "big data" in 2018, Albert-László Barabási may have discovered a huge part of it. More about Barabási's research in a future chapter.

Like Hill, I grew up in poverty in the geographic center of the Appalachian Mountains. My parents made sure we were never without adequate food (mostly from the garden), clothing (mostly used or hand-me-downs), and shelter with running water (though no toilet in the bathroom). Note: My parents were able to afford to have a well drilled and to purchase a water heater, but they didn't have enough money to install a septic tank—the municipal sewer didn't extend that far out. People still comment that my mother kept the floors in our house so clean that you could literally eat off them despite working overtime at a sewing factory for minimum wage. Not having much caused me to think a great deal about achieving success, which for me at the time meant becoming rich. Recent research suggests that being rich is *not* highly correlated with success or happiness! At an early age, I figured that two ways to become successful *financially* were to: (1) work hard and (2) save money and let my money "work" for me.

In 1971, when I was 13 years old, Virginia law stated that a person had to be 15 years and 10 months old to get a work permit—so I became an entrepreneur! I started mowing lawns at an average of $1.50 a yard—the same amount as minimum wage per hour that both my parents earned, delivering newspapers at 5 cents profit per paper, selling items door-to-door on a route, and by mail order/direct marketing! Since my expenses were low, I started saving money.

My mail order business was profitable soon after starting, but it wasn't extremely successful. I learned later from professionals in the industry that I had done a lot of things right that most beginners didn't. I learned a great deal about that business segment, and when online, internet or digital marketing began to proliferate, I was already miles ahead in that game! Even during my youth, I recognized that personal success and entrepreneurship were highly correlated—and years later I discovered that personal success and leadership and happiness were also connected.

The day I turned 15 years and 10 months old, I went to my high school principal's office, got my work permit, and took a different bus to "downtown" Norton, Virginia—the Commonwealth's smallest independent city with a population in 1973 of 5,000 people. At the first place that I applied for a job (F. W. Woolworth), the manager was so impressed with my eagerness to learn and *willingness* to do any work that he hired me on the spot! The salary was minimum wage—in 1973, $1.60 per hour—and my duties included cleaning the store, stocking shelves, assembling products—particularly bicycles—and assisting all the other employees in whatever was needed. I still tell my students that I learned more about marketing from the manager of that F. W. Woolworth in those three years of part-time work than I ever did in all my college courses, including the doctoral marketing courses!

Five years after reading *Think and Grow Rich,* I "accidently" created a holistic and synergistic theory/model of success based on secondary research utilizing a pyramid of four sciences—physiology, psychology, sociology, and philosophy. I integrated Hill's principles or traits into the four sides of my pyramid model. But even then, I knew something was missing from my model. For many years, I read and evaluated hundreds of success books and collected thousands of articles that strengthened the validity of my theory/model. But I still was

WHY IT IS IMPORTANT TO STUDY "SUCCESS" | 27

unable to find exactly what was missing—until now! And it is more than I ever imagined!

Wouldn't it be great if a theory or formula could be developed that could account for say 50 percent or more of those who try it becoming not only successful but *authentically* so? Perhaps Napoleon Hill didn't discover all the *necessary* traits for success, or perhaps adding another theory or two or more theories would account for a larger percentage of people becoming successful. By combining many theories that each account for a little success with many other theories from diverse disciplines and utilizing the research accumulated over many centuries, I've been able to arrive at a formula that results in a significantly larger percentage of people becoming successful.

The simple model/theory I created in 1976 is shown in Figure 1. I used the pyramid shape because if one side gets too much out of balance, the entire pyramid could collapse. Another reason was I sensed that the pyramid shape could be an energy-generating machine, and that Nikola Tesla was correct when he theorized that the pyramids of Egypt could store and move electricity. Moreover, Tesla theorized that the materials used to construct the pyramids had properties that allowed them to trap enormous amounts of energy from the sun and moon that could light up entire cities, run machines, and even be used for healing.[2]

My formula for personal success was Success = (Physiology + Psychology + Sociology + Philosophy) X Balance or the

---

2. "Tesla Uncovered the Ancient Mystery of the Pyramids"; https://brightside.me/articles/tesla-uncovered-the-ancient-mystery-of-the-pyramids-814494/; accessed January 6, 2025.

summation of the four sides of the pyramid, utilizing a 10-point scale for each, times balance with a score of 2 – 10 with 10 being all four sides perfectly balanced. A perfect score would be 400 [(10 + 10 + 10 + 10) X 10 = 400]. An average score of 5 on all four sides of the pyramid and a 10 for balance would result in a score of 200. Should one side be more than one point higher than one of the other three sides, then two points would be subtracted from the balance score. So, a (5 + 5 + 5 + 7) X 8 would be only 176 points or less than if all four sides were balanced.

Figure 1: Original Model/Theory

My original model/theory titled the Personal Marketing Pyramid (1976; 1988):

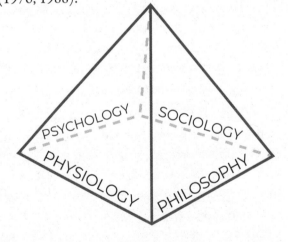

You may be struggling with the fundamentals of success and especially "authentic success." You may have some concept of what it means and maybe even some vague idea of general principles but aren't clear on how to implement them. And that's where all the advice out there is insufficient: it's easy to represent the end goal, harder to provide a clear path. And that's what I'm offering you here: scientific rigor to complement the vision.

HOW THE BOOK IS LAID OUT

This book has six chapters in addition to this Introduction and a Conclusion. In Chapter 1, I examine 12 terms—from "self-improvement" to "personal branding"—that are used as alternative or substitute words for "success." These terms were defined and key words from these definitions were extracted and examined via content analysis to determine the term that best describes the essence of what success truly is and to determine traits of successful people. From this research, a new formula for success was refined by identifying a three-step process and discovering the concepts that would form the base of the pyramid—the idea or opportunity.

Next, I examine 45 definitions—many by notable people who are considered successful. Utilizing a content analysis of the key words in these definitions, I arrived at an operational definition of success. Then I enhanced this definition by examining numerous success rules, keys, elements, and causes found online. Although most of these rules or keys were not based on scientific research, several concepts were quite logical, and I realized they needed to be included in the definition and subsequent formula/model. Finally, I compare the key words in my definition with the findings of another researcher and added several additional key words.

In Chapter 2, I present a brief review of more than 40 possible theories of success and explain why most separately don't work very well. In the process of discussing these theories, I discovered several that could be added to the life balance and trait theories associated with my pyramid. These additional theories, though not very effective alone, in combination assisted me in creating my comprehensive theory/model for authentic success.

In Chapter 3, I do a deep dive into the literature regarding the life balance theory of success, since it is an important part of my theory and now has some empirical support. Also, I discuss the contributions of the many researchers who championed the life balance theory or a similar idea. Finally, I discuss why life balance alone isn't enough for most people to achieve true, authentic, and sustainable success.

In Chapter 4, I return to Napoleon Hill's trait theory and other researchers who have cataloged traits of successful people. Utilizing what I learned from Chapter 1, I compare Hill's findings with several recent trait theories of success. Further, I argue for the combination of life balance theory (Chapter 3) and trait theory and explain why the combination still isn't enough for most people to achieve true or authentic success.

In Chapter 5, I review a sample of 24 existing success formulas. Then, I make an amazing discovery! Moreover, I discuss the top traits common to all four sides of my pyramid model and how to use these traits for authentic success. Then, I present the new formula/model/theory of success based on the findings arrived at in Chapter 1, an integration of several of the theories discussed in Chapter 2, and the combination of both the life balance (Chapter 3) and trait (Chapter 4) theories. Finally, I discuss the interaction effects in this formula.

In Chapter 6, I present a "deeper" dive into the four major components of the new formula. First, I give evidence for "love"—including generosity, gratitude, giving, and receiving—as being the most important trait in all four sides of the pyramid. Second, I discuss the vital importance of recognizing and seizing opportunities or great ideas by doing a deeper dive into the model I outlined in Chapter 1. Moreover, I explain how to empirically evaluate whether an opportunity or idea is right for a person and why scalability and passion are the most crucial components. Finally, research findings about why the idea must be unique, satisfy a need, be priced for value and other considerations are shared. Third, I explain why visualizing the completion of SMART goals, intentions or promises is crucial to success and why it alone is not enough. Fourth, I discuss in more detail why taking action—either massive or micro—is essential.

Finally, I close by drawing conclusions regarding success as a journey and authentic versus material success.

But to understand how authentic success is a science that can be tested and applied, we must start by defining it...

CHAPTER 1

I KNOW IT WHEN I SEE IT

Determining, Defining, and Developing
"Success Science" for You

For many years, researchers have been trying to explain what success is and what it's not. Some argue that what constitutes success is different for every person, and as such, it cannot be defined. Nevertheless, if we could determine a definition of success—especially authentic success—we could then work toward developing a formula that will result in more people becoming successful!

There exists a simple research tool that could result in making progress toward determining both the best term to describe success and an operational definition of it. That tool is *content analysis,* which is used to study the presence of certain words, themes, or concepts and their relationships within some given qualitative data set. Doing this exercise will also reveal some crucial traits researchers have determined are associated with success.

THE TERM "SUCCESS" IS A SEMANTIC JUNGLE

Success is known by many names, including: (1) self-improvement; (2) self-help; (3) self-care; (4) self-development; (5) self-leadership; (6) self-management; (7) life management; (8) personal management; (9) personal marketing; (10) personal achievement; (11) personal development; and (12) personal branding. These are all just terms for essentially the same concept. To see the full context for my content analysis of these terms, visit the book's website— https://thesuccesspyramid .com/.

A summative content analysis of the key words revealed that only four of the 12 terms' definitions contained key words mentioned more than four times. In order of most to least, these key words were: (1) continuous improvement, (2) resources, (3) actions, and (4) goals. The major finding from this exercise is that these key words imply that each side of my original pyramid model—physiology, psychology, sociology, philosophy—interacts with at least three components: goals, resources, and actions. Goals lead us to examine resources, which lead to actions that result in "continuous improvement," generating new goals—and the process continues.

Many researchers argue that the starting point should be resources, since this often limits what you can achieve. However, my research indicates that you should first set goals before examining your resources. If you set lofty goals, you could always borrow, beg, or steal (though the latter is not advised) sufficient resources to achieve them.

Figure 1.1: Goals, Resources, Actions Interaction

Figure 1.1 shows how goals, resources, and actions interact with the sides of my original pyramid model/theory (2024):

Two additional variables are implied. Research has confirmed what Napoleon Hill found around 1930 that "success begins in the form of an *intense* desire." So, desire comes before goals. Moreover, Hill states, "It has been said, and not without reason, that one may have anything one wants, within reasonable limitations, providing one wants it badly enough!" Hill goes on to say that "wishing for a thing is not the same as desiring it with such intensity that out of this desire grow impelling forces of action which drive one to build plans and put those plans to work." Finally, Hill notes that "most people never advance beyond the wishing stage." So, you must have a burning desire for something to achieve it. If your desire is only "warm," then you won't have the motivation to gather resources and act. Note that it is highly likely that a burning desire is just another term for a definite goal, intention, or promise.

It is possible that another variable comes into play. That variable, habits, would go after actions. According to James Clear in his book *Atomic Habits,* you can achieve any goal by developing good habits.

So, if you want to become successful, develop SMART (specific, measurable, achievable, relevant, and time-bound)[3] goals[4] and then take micro and/or massive actions to achieve these desired goals. This process should be repeated for each of the four sides of the pyramid.

For example, for physiology you might have a burning desire to lose weight. Resources such as money could be utilized to purchase an effective diet program, home exercise equipment, and a gym membership. Sticking with the program and going regularly to the gym (persistence) would be the "action" part for this side of the pyramid.

You can work on multiple goals for each side of the pyramid at the same time, as long as your efforts are focused. Plato said that Socrates believed that we give the most attention to the least important things and the least attention to the most important things. I am guilty of this, especially when dealing

---

3. See George T. Doran, "There's a S.M.A.R.T. Way to Write Management's Goals and Objectives," Management Review, November 1981.

4. Or "intentions" as one researcher argues and I wholeheartedly agree or "promises" as another author calls goals or "burning desires" as Napoleon Hill terms them regarding the utilization of your resources, including those you borrow or exchange for more appropriate resources.

with "small" money matters. For instance, I spent many hours getting a $14 refund. This can be prevented by determining which goals are the most important for you to achieve authentic success and not dedicating too much time and effort to less important ones.

My goals changed after I received a cancer diagnosis that was likely terminal. Before cancer, my goals were numerous and included things like more money, a lake home, fame, travel, and publishing a novel. After learning I had one of the deadliest forms of cancer, my goals became more authentic, such as helping as many people as possible achieve authentic success and leaving a legacy. I realized that I already had enough money, though I suppose everyone wants more; had traveled all over the world, though not to every place I had desired; and that a big house and more material possessions would not make my life more meaningful.

Once you determine your goals, then you can direct resources toward them. Research shows that the more resources you have, the easier it is to become successful. At the same time, massive resources don't guarantee success. If you have lots of resources, you can buy things that enhance success. However, some success components cannot be purchased, such as motivation, persistence, and gratitude. You should also note that certain variables, including genetics and luck, often play a role in determining whether you will become successful regardless of the resources that you command.

Further, research indicates that many individuals with few or modest resources achieve great success. Oftentimes, the traits that are highly correlated with success require merely time for study or deliberate practice—and time is the *only* resource of which you and I get an equal amount every day. Nevertheless, it should be noted that with money, you can purchase "time" in the form of time-saving devices and labor assistance.

Analyzing the terms and definitions confirmed that success is a process of utilizing and improving or exchanging resources (i.e., skills, talents, traits, capabilities, experiences, potentialities). These resources are enhanced most effectively via:

(1) Motivation and aspiration resulting in definite and specific goals

(2) Action involving intention, deliberate practice, effort, hard work, continuous improvement, achievement, and progress, including small wins while overcoming obstacles and failures

(3) Building responsible habits that result in a positive outlook, higher quality of life, greater well-being, and happiness

Actions can be micro or massive as long as they result in continuous improvement. Moreover, actions should lead to new *good* habits. I considered making habits a fourth component for success in my pyramid model. However, Linda and Richard Eyre in their book *Lifebalance: How to Simplify and Bring Harmony to Your Everyday Life* write, "The easiest number of areas to balance is *three*. It's relatively easy to juggle three balls, whereas four are many times more difficult."[5] Since I already had three variables on each side of the four sides of the pyramid, I didn't feel I could add more variables to "juggle."

---

5. Linda and Richard Eyre, *Lifebalance: How to Simplify and Bring Harmony to Your Everyday Life* (Touchstone, 1997), 64.

Therefore, which of these interchangeable terms is the most appropriate to call this discipline or field of study? "Self-development," with four key words, would seem to be the best term to use in lieu of success. "Personal achievement" would be the second best, with three key words. Five of the 12 terms had two key words, while three had one, and two—personal management and personal marketing—had none.

Ironically, an extensive search revealed that neither the No. 1 term "self-development" nor the No. 2 term "personal achievement" were in any recent book titles. Moreover, not a single recent book published had the words "personal management" or "personal marketing" in the title, though Internet searches on these topics generated quite lengthy lists. Note that many of the hits on "personal management" were for "personnel management," as in human resources. However, the term "success" was in numerous book titles! This supports the idea that the term "success" should be utilized instead of one of the other 11 terms.

Nevertheless, it appears to be merely a personal choice or semantics as a rational argument can be made for any of these interchangeable terms as being the most appropriate to call this field of study. The term "self-help" may be too broad. For example, I ordered a 596-page book titled *Self-Help that Works*, published by Oxford University Press. While it was an informative and useful book, it contained only 12 pages about success as it is being studied for this book.

A closer examination of all 12 terms reveals that all are to some degree limiting, as several are mostly used in specific fields such as (1) self-care in nursing, (2) life management in psychology, and (3) personal branding in marketing. The

I KNOW IT WHEN I SEE IT | 39

content analysis confirms that none of the 12 terms *completely* capture what most researchers denote as success. Therefore, the term "success" should be utilized.

A NEW DEFINITION OF SUCCESS

Now that we know that the word "success" is probably the best term to describe the construct, I'm going to use it throughout this book. Next, having an operational definition—we already have numerous conceptual definitions—is crucial before success can become a science. Ask 100 people their definition of success and you will probably get 100 different responses. As early as 1969, Richard Weiss wrote in his book *The American Myth of Success: From Horatio Alger to Norman Vincent Peale,* "Any student of the success myth encounters the seemingly insoluble dilemma of finding any consistent definition of success. At different times, it seems to mean virtue, money [wealth], happiness, or a combination of all three."[6]

While several researchers have suggested that wealth equals success and success is equal to happiness, recent research is clear: wealth, if it has any relationship at all to success, is most likely a by-product, while happiness seems to come *before* success! Earl Nightingale recounts a study in his book *The Strangest Secret: How to Live the Life You Desire* about 100 people who started even at age 25. By age 65, 36 of them had died and only one

---

6. Richard Weiss, *The American Myth of Success: From Horatio Alger to Norman Vincent Peale* (University of Illinois Press, 1988 reprint), 15.

had become rich and four were financially independent. So based on this study, only 5 percent became successful.

It is true that my new formula will result in you "getting anything you desire," including becoming rich. According to October 2024 data from the Federal Reserve, the median net worth of US households overall is $192,900. The top 2 percent of Americans have a net worth of about $2.472 million, while the top 5 percent have a net worth of around $1.03 million. I've been very blessed to be in this top percentage, though I started out in 1980 with a minus $800 net worth!

But apparently, I did everything right—or mostly right—regarding creating wealth, including:

1. *Setting and achieving financial goals*—one of my goals was to be a millionaire by the time I was 30. I achieved this, but I think I was in my early 30s!

2. *Saving money*—I saved small amounts early on in my career, but as my income increased, so did my savings.

3. *Spending less than I earned*—I spent substantially less than I earned especially by cutting out many unnecessary expenses, such as paying interest or late fees.

4. *Living below my means and being debt-free*—most of my life, by choice, I lived well below my means and was debt-free much of the time.

I KNOW IT WHEN I SEE IT | 41

5. *Investing my savings*—I bought and sold real estate, invested in the stock market, and created small businesses.

6. *Tithing and/or contributing to charitable causes*—this was and continues to be my "best" investment. My goal is to donate 50 percent of my income to charitable causes each year. I don't always do it, however. I initiated this goal many years ago when I read the 1968 Og Mandino book *The Greatest Salesman in the World*. I heard a preacher on the radio use as an example a man who gives away 90 percent of his income and lives on the 10 percent. I'm not there yet!

7. *Preparing for retirement*—beginning at age 50, I faithfully added extra money to my retirement accounts. For example, the 401(k) contribution limit for 2024 was $23,000 for employee salary deferrals, but for those age 50 or older, there was an additional $7,500 in catch-up contributions, raising the deferral limit to $30,500.

However, it is my hope that you seek *authentic* success and not just wealth, fame, or material possessions.

My task of defining "success" was much more daunting than I would have ever imagined! While I am confident that "I know success when I see it," I spent over a year trying to arrive at an operational definition that could be utilized for empirical research.

Though you may have a different idea of what success is and how to achieve it, a comprehensive definition can be constructed—by utilizing content analysis.

As mentioned, success researchers disagree passionately about what should be included (i.e., goals, action, love) or not be included (i.e., money, fame, power, being admired) in a definition. Indeed, some researchers argue that an operational definition is not necessary at all. I and many others disagree, because you can't measure something without an operational definition of it! Regardless of how good your conceptual definition might be, a person really needs an empirical basis to know when success has been achieved.

I collected definitions of "success" by people who, by all measures, could wear that badge, and extracted a list of the key words from their definitions. The resulting table can be found in Appendix A. From most to least frequent, these key words were:

- Actions
- Resources
- Life satisfaction
- Failures
- Continuous improvement
- Goals
- Happiness
- Well-being
- Ideas/opportunities
- Exchanging

- Balance
- Process
- Benefit of others
- Risks
- Planning

"Actions" was the concept most often mentioned (14 times) as being a key word that should be included in a definition of success. While almost all models include actions as a core variable, I've found a few well-known success models whose creators argue that actions are not necessary, notably Rhonda Byrne in her book *The Secret* and other "New Age" tomes. In his book *Take the Stairs: 7 Steps to Achieving True Success*, Rory Vaden wrote:

> The popular book and movie *The Secret* teaches us that we create our lives with every thought of every minute of every day. Yes, this is true and I [Vaden—though I, Caudill, do as well] believe in the concept and practice it every day—but if we don't get off our butts and take action, we won't achieve anything. The real secret to success has more to do with *action* than *attraction*. We just don't talk about it as much because it doesn't sell as well.

"Resources" was second (mentioned 10 times). In addition to time and money, resources may be categorized as physiological, psychological, sociological (emotional) or philosophical (my original pyramid theory/model). While "Life satisfaction" was third (8 times) and "Failures" fourth (7 times), I don't think they need separate categories. Perhaps "Life satisfaction" could be included in the "Goals" section since all worthy goals should lead to life satisfaction.

Because all social sciences involve a "process," I include it in my definition, even though only one person in the sample mentioned it specifically. Finally, no person in my sample group mentioned "risks" or "planning," but it is well known that achieving any goal or intention involves both. Even though "exchange" received only one mention, I consider it a critical variable since in every case a resource must be given up to obtain another resource or an increase in one or another. For instance, the resource of time can be expended on learning a new skill, or the resource of money can be spent on courses or materials to enhance an existing trait.

Finally, "Ideas/opportunities" had only one mention. However, Barabási (2018) found that the quality of the "random idea" represented half of his success formula. Barabási and his team checked and re-checked their data. Since I have a lot of confidence in Barabási's methodology and findings, I'm adding to my definition six factors that make an idea "quality":

- Scalability
- Passion
- Uniqueness
- Serves a definite need or desire
- Value priced
- Other
  - desirable

I KNOW IT WHEN I SEE IT | 45

- feasible
- viable
- simple
- innovative
- impactable
- original
- designed to solve a problem

An idea or opportunity can be quite unique and yet not be successful because the market simply does not exist for it or it can't be value priced, which is sometimes hard to do. Of course, there can be other variables that impact the potency of an idea or opportunity, depending on its nature.

In Figure 1.2, the base of my pyramid represents the potential value of an idea and the importance of recognizing and seizing opportunities or ideas. The "idea" is illustrated by the small center circle and the variables that contribute to the quality of the idea surround this circle as slices. The two large slices represent: (1) scalability which no idea in the world today can be very successful without a high ability to scale—it has been said you must "scale or fail"; and (2) passion which no idea can be very successful without a person having a high level of passion for it.

If you have great ideas for which you are *not* genuinely passionate about, consider: (1) "selling" the idea to someone who is ardent about it; (2) trading it; (3) leasing it; or (4) giving it away (i.e., to a non-profit organization or to a for-profit firm to establish "good will"). The idea will never be successful if you are less than passionate about it.

Figure 1.2: Base of Original Pyramid

The following figure, conceived in 2024, depicts the base, or idea component, of my original Pyramid Model/Theory.

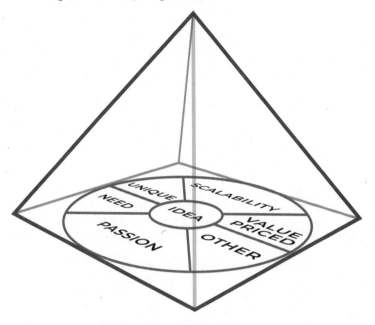

The remaining "slices" in Figure 1.2 are for the idea to: (1) be unique; (2) serve a definite need or desire for at least one large target market or audience; (3) have the ability to be value priced; and (4) an "other" component which will vary depending on the nature of the idea or opportunity. An idea can be quite unique and yet not be successful because there are no or too small of a market for it, not much need or desire, or it can't be value priced which is sometimes hard to do. Note that the "other" slice contains additional variables that are often important in determining if an idea will be feasible, profitable, or demanded.

One recent article listed seven variables: (1) Clarity; (2) Usability; (3) Stability; (4) Scalability; (5) Stickiness; (6) Integration; and (7) Profitability. While my model incorporates usability, scalability, and profitability, clarity, stability, and integration are implied. I love the notion of stickiness which the authors—professors at Cornell University—admit is like usability. The distinction is, "Can the idea become a habit or trend ('stick')?"

In the book *Made to Stick: Why Some Ideas Survive and Others Die* (2007), authors Chip and Dan Heath write, "As we poured over hundreds of sticky ideas, we saw, over and over, the same six principles." These principles were:

1. *Simplicity*—you must make your idea simple by stripping it down to its core.

2. *Unexpectedness*—you must generate interest and curiosity.

3. *Concreteness*—you must explain your ideas in sensory language; words or phrases that appeal to the five senses of sight, sound, smell, taste, and touch, which allows others to vividly imagine a scene or experience.

4. *Credibility*—you must emphasize the credentials of your idea.

5. *Emotions*—you must make people feel something about your idea. (The Heaths write, "Research shows that people are more likely to make a

charitable gift to a single needy individual than to an entire impoverished region. We are wired to feel things for people, not for abstractions.")

6. *Stories*—you must tell stories about your ideas as it helps people remember you or your product or service better. In addition, the authors note that you will have to discard of lot of great ideas to "let the most important insight shine."

Because there are too many potential definitions for the concept of success, I'm going to limit my definition to authentic, true, or sustainable success. Based on the key words in the sampling of definitions of success, I propose the following definition of success:

> True, Authentic or Sustainable Success is the process of recognizing and seizing quality ideas/opportunities that are scalable, unique, needful, demanded, value priced and that you are passionate about and planning and exchanging resources, including physiological, psychological, sociological (emotional) and philosophical, to achieve an ambitious, holistic, and balanced array of focused goals, intentions, promises or visions by assuming risks, overcoming failures, and enthusiastically taking actions that enhance continuous improvement and positively influence target audiences' life satisfaction, well-being, and happiness.

I KNOW IT WHEN I SEE IT | 49

I did a separate content analysis of the various definitions of personal branding which was one of the alternate terms for success. The actual table is on the book's website— https://thesuccesspyramid.com/. The majority of the key words were the same as for authentic success, but there were two major differences—differentiation and positioning. Typically, successful people have made themselves distinct and stand out in some way from those who are considered failures. The concepts of value added, leverage across platforms, and consistent message and image uncovered during the content analysis of personal branding could also be variables that could be included in a new definition of success.

ENHANCING THE DEFINITION OF SUCCESS

To further validate this definition, I conducted research online between April and June 2022 regarding what had been written about success and found support for all the variables in the above definition and more! After reviewing 31 online articles (see Appendix B), it became clear that an additional 22 variables should be included in my definition of success. These were:

1. Preparation

2. Visualize, being able to

3. Challenging

4. Time

5. Money

6. Belief

7. Differentiation

8. Determination

9. Massive actions

10. Discipline

11. Habits

12. Perseverance

13. Value-added

14. Positioning

15. Not becoming complacent

16. Hard but enjoyable work (deliberate practice)

17. Love self, mind, others, and a higher power

18. Healthy body, mind, and soul

19. Self-confidence

20. Self-control

21. Positive attitude

22. Stay curious

Although not in any online definition I could find, having "quiet time" and the "help of others" (i.e., having mentors was mentioned one time) were deemed crucial by several prominent researchers on achieving success. Therefore, I have added these two variables. The enhanced definition of success (with additions in *italics*) is as follows:

> True, Authentic or Sustainable Success is the process through (1) *"quiet time," hard but enjoyable work, the help of others, staying curious, and love of self, mind, others, and a higher power* of (2) recognizing and seizing quality ideas/opportunities that are scalable, unique, needful, demanded, value priced, and that you are passionate about, (3) planning, *preparing,* and exchanging resources including *time, money, belief (faith),* physiological, psychological, sociological (emotional) and philosophical to (4) *position* an ambitious, holistic, *differentiated* and balanced array of focused, *challenging, visualized* and *value-added* "written" SMART goals, *intentions, promises,* or visions by (5) assuming risk(s), (6) overcoming failure(s), being persistent and *persevering,* (7) taking enthusiastic, *massive* (or

numerous micro), *determined* actions that (8) enhance continuous improvement, (9) develop *disciplined habits including a healthy body, mind and soul* and (10) positively influence you and your target audiences' life-satisfaction, well-being, fun and happiness (11) *with self-confidence, self-control and a positive attitude without becoming complacent.*

Yes, that is a mouthful! But this definition includes nearly all elements, components, aspects or traits of success and personal branding. Knowing these major variables can enable you to become proactive in creating or enhancing your own success. And preparing this definition has solidified the foundation of my new success formula.

The book *Do the Right Thing, Do it All the Time: 75 Success Secrets Listed for Fast Reference* by Frank Leigh contains 75 practical keys or secrets to success listed alphabetically and explained in a few paragraphs each. Leigh states that these secrets were taken from hundreds of success and happiness books. The summary on Amazon about Leigh's book states: "You can research success and happiness for many years, reading every book you can find on the subject, but at some point you realize they are basically all teaching the same things, just in different ways and have been doing so for thousands of years. That's when you have to put it all together and decide what could actually work for you here and now; and what could be helpful at other stages in life."

Therefore, I compared the 75 "secrets" from this book with the concepts included in my "scientific" definition of success.

Nearly one-third (24) of the concepts were the same or very similar. This supports Leigh's theory that success researchers are "basically all teaching the same things." Notably, Leigh did not find the importance of: (1) "quiet time"; (2) exchange; (3) positioning; (4) success being holistic; (5) differentiation; (6) balance; (7) value-added; (8) passion; (9) vision; (10) continuous improvement; (11) without becoming complacent; and (12) staying curious. All of these concepts have scientific proof, but several might have been discovered after Leigh published his book in 2018. However, I found 14 concepts from this book that were not in my definition but have scientific support. I've added these to the definition below in **bold.**

> True, Authentic or Sustainable Success is the process (1) through **choices, simplicity, imagination,** "quiet time," hard but enjoyable work **that results in "flow,"** staying curious, the help of others **and reciprocity,** and love of self, mind, others, and a higher power of (2) recognizing and seizing quality ideas/opportunities that are scalable, unique, needful, demanded, value priced, and that you are passionate about, (3) planning, preparing, and exchanging resources including time, money, belief (faith), physiological, psychological, sociological (emotional) and philosophical to (4) position an ambitious, holistic, differentiated and balanced array of focused, challenging, visualized and value-added "written" SMART goals, intentions, promises, or visions by (5) assuming risk(s), (6) overcoming

fears, challenges, stressors, weaknesses, negative thoughts, failure(s), being persistent and persevering, (7) taking enthusiastic, massive (or numerous micro), determined actions that (8) enhance continuous improvement, (9) develop disciplined habits including a healthy body, mind and soul and (10) positively influence you and your target audiences' life-satisfaction, well-being, fun and happiness (11) with self-confidence, self-control, **self-discipline, forgiveness, giving back, gratitude,** and a positive attitude without becoming complacent.

This definition of 168 words becomes more manageable when these factors are categorized into four areas, as illustrated by the simple pyramid model I created in 1976. This will be done in Chapter 5 after all or most all of the scientifically documented traits of successful people are identified. I selected the pyramid shape because research showed that to be successful overall in any endeavor, project, plan or even one's life, a person has to balance the component parts. A pyramid could collapse if one side gets significantly out of balance. Each of the four sides have a score of 1 to 10 points with 10 being perfect. The balance score ranges from 2 to 10 with two points being deducted for each of the four variables for each more than one point different from the other. For example, if a person scores 9, 8, 7, 5, then their balance score would be 8. Using this model, a person can quickly see if a side is out of balance and take steps to correct it. But as will be shown in Chapter 3, this

I KNOW IT WHEN I SEE IT | 55

model represented only about one-fourth of my new formula for *authentic* success.

In addition to identifying numerous traits of successful people, these exercises have also revealed that a hierarchy exists in the process. This consists of exchanging and utilizing resources, identifying and creating goals, intentions or promises and taking actions from micro to massive. Finally, these content analyses revealed that the idea would be the base of the pyramid.

Now, let's examine some theories that could be added to my existing life balance and trait pyramid theory that could increase the percentage of people using my new formula in becoming successful.

CHAPTER 2

THE BLIND MEN AND THE ELEPHANT

A Brief Review of Incomplete Success Theories

A group of blind men heard that a strange animal, called an elephant, had been brought to the town, but none of them were aware of its shape and form. Out of curiosity, they said: "We must inspect and know it by touch, of which we are capable." So, they sought it out, and when they found it, they groped about it. The first person, whose hand landed on the trunk, said, "This being is like a thick snake." For another one whose hand reached its ear, it seemed like a kind of fan. As for another person, whose hand was upon its leg, said the elephant is a pillar like a tree-trunk. The blind man who placed his hand upon its side said the elephant "is a wall." Another who felt its tail, described it as a rope.

The last felt its tusk, stating the elephant is that which is hard, smooth and like a spear.[7]

Existing theories of success are like the six blind men touching different parts of the elephant in this Hindu parable (this same parable can be found in the Buddha's teaching). Just as each blind man describes the elephant based on his *partial* experience, success theorists have created different theories/models/formulas based on their *partial* or personal experience or limited research. And just as all the blind men's theories of what an elephant looks like are equally true, though none are complete, so are those of success researchers! However, each existing theory/model/formula for success results in only a small percentage of people who faithfully follow the prescribed method/philosophy becoming successful.

The problem is *not* that the existing success theories are wrong. *All* actually work—for *some* people, usually a small percentage, including the author. Like with the men touching different parts of the elephant and claiming absolute truth, success researchers have written explanations based on their limited, subjective experience as they ignore other people's limited, subjective experiences that may be equally true. It is also very likely that existing theories of success do not include all the critical variables or, more likely, include spurious factors.

---

7. From C.R. Snyder and Carol E. Ford, eds., Coping with Negative Life Events: Clinical and Social Psychological Perspectives (Springer Science + Business Media, 2013). And E. Bruce Goldstein, *Encyclopedia of Perception* (SAGE Publications, 2010), 492.

The following is a brief discussion of quite a few of the various theories of success (though not all), the advantages of and problem(s) with them, and why each alone doesn't work very well. This categorization and illumination of various theories has resulted in the creation of a more robust, complementary, and scientific theory of the science of success. Let's start with the most common existing theories of success—the life balance and trait theories.

LIFE BALANCE THEORY

As you will discover in Chapter 3, the life balance theory of success is compelling. According to Kathleen Matuska in her 2016 book *Life Balance: Science and Stories of Everyday Living*, "Life balance seems to be a legitimate, scientific construct, different from other constructs like life satisfaction and quality of life. This finding is a big deal because only recently has life balance had any scientific support."

Moreover, the "life balance" theory of success is not new, even though currently it is receiving a lot of renewed interest. Life balance has been practiced since ancient times. Indeed, over 2,500 years ago, Euripides (484 BC–406 BC) wrote, "The best and safest thing is to keep a *balance* in your life…. If you can do that, and live that way, you are really a wise man [person]." Even though researchers have known for a long time the importance of balance in our lives, only a handful of formulas and models have been developed to measure life balance and its relationship to success.

Life balance is the concept of managing the different segments of life with the goal of equilibrium and creating synergy—two or more life segments producing a combined effect greater than the sum of their separate effects. In Chapter 3, I do a content analysis on some various life balance models. Several of these life balance models utilized four categories, but several others had five or more components. However, the results indicated that all the factors could be included in the four sides of my original pyramid model, which was a combination of about 75 percent life balance (four specific categories of resources need to be in harmony for true or authentic success to manifest) and about 25 percent trait theory (each side of the pyramid contained specific traits that needed to be balanced).

TRAIT THEORY

For a deep dive into numerous "trait" models/theories of success (from Aristotle to Benjamin Franklin to modern-day researchers), see Chapter 4. Traits are sometimes called talents, skills, abilities, habits, principles, virtues, assets, or strengths, and many books have been written using each term. This theory, which suggests that successful people have specific traits in common, has been a favorite of success researchers ever since Napoleon Hill published his "scientific" *Law of Success* book in 1928, which he based on more than 500 interviews of successful people and thousands of failures (Hill claimed these questionnaires were later destroyed in a fire).

RESOURCES MANAGEMENT THEORY

This theory, in the context of the science of success, is my adaptation of trait theory, in which the term "resources" is applied instead of traits because some resources such as money and time are not exactly traits. However, "good time management" or "saving money" could be. Note that "a habit of saving" was one of Napoleon Hill's original traits. My definition of integrated resource management is the planning, organizing, and allocation of physiological, psychological, sociological, and philosophical resources—including time and money—to achieve sustainable goals.

CONCENTRATED RESOURCES THEORY

Building on the former, this theory (Caudill created in 2024) maintains that success is more likely to happen when resources are plentiful (including time and money). However, many people have failed at achieving goals even though they had little or no financial or time constraints. Nevertheless, more of a trait does seem to have a positive effect on outcomes. For instance, attractive people get paid more, get considered for more jobs and promotions, and have stronger social skills than unattractive people. Also, having an abundance of charisma—the ability to motivate others through charm, persuasiveness, and interpersonal connection—can result in success more rapidly. And just as physical attractiveness and charisma are moderate and persistent predictors of success, having a lot of time and money to devote to attaining goals may make success easier and/or more feasible. Note that while charisma is a trait that can be learned, physical attractiveness for the most part is determined by a person's DNA. However, you can make yourself more attractive in several ways including smiling more often!

CONTINUOUS COMPOUNDING THEORY

I maintain that each of the four sides of my success pyramid are "accounts" containing various resources (Caudill created in 2024). This means that a person can enjoy the continuous growth of their resources (talents, skills, abilities, habits, principles, virtues, assets, or strengths) like earning interest in a savings account monthly, quarterly, or annually with regular compounding. According to James Clear in his book *Atomic Habits*, "If you get one percent better each day for one year, you'll end up thirty-seven times better by the time you're done. This is why small choices [actions] don't make much of a difference at the time but add up over the long-term."

SMALL WINS THEORY

Similar to the Continuous Compounding Theory, this theory holds that seemingly insignificant minor choices (actions) can have large consequences. The Pareto Distribution—sometimes called the 80/20 rule—often applies to success attainment. The principle states that, for many events, roughly 80 percent of the effects come from 20 percent of the causes. It's an uneven distribution that can be found in countless life and business situations. So, 80 percent of an image problem might be the result of something as simple as not smiling enough!

ANTHROPIC THEORY

This theory is like baby bear's oatmeal in the Goldilocks story needing to be "just right!" Conditions (the environment) must be "just right" for success, too. If the "observed value" of just one essential condition (resource) is off even a little in either direction (too much or too little), that person will not succeed.

ICEBERG THEORY

This is basically trait theory in that the idea of what is "seen" (the iceberg) is only about 20 percent of what it actually takes (traits) to succeed (the other 80 percent is "ice" hidden below the water's surface). Success is like this in that numerous traits that empirically impact authentic success are not overt.

LUCK THEORY

Some researchers believe people become successful because they are lucky enough to be in the "right place at the right time" or lucky enough to have somebody backing them such as a great mentor, devoted loved one, or significant other. Conversely, bad luck results in failure(s). See for example Michael J. Mauboussin's book *The Success Equation: Untangling Skill and Luck in Business, Sports, and Investing.*

ATTRIBUTION THEORY

Several researchers have suggested that most successful people don't really know what made them successful! Therefore, people look for explanations or causes that can be attributed to their own success or failure. An assumption of the attribution theory is that people will interpret their environment in such a way as to maintain a positive self-image. It has been demonstrated that causal attributions impact the likelihood of undertaking success activities, the intensity of work at these activities, and the degree of persistence in the face of failure.

HAPPY ACCIDENTS THEORY

Related to luck theory, many people say their success was merely the result of fortuitous events that occurred by chance or serendipity—unexpected good luck in finding good things without looking for them. For more on this, see Morton A. Meyers' *Happy Accidents.* However, "happy accidents" are almost always a result of finding something useful in another area *while working on something else.*

ROTA FORTUNAE (WHEEL OF FORTUNE) THEORY

Some researchers argue that success is just random, like the turning of a wheel. The wheel belongs to the goddess Fortuna who spins it at random (often blindfolded), changing the positions of those on the wheel: some suffer great misfortune; others gain windfalls. This theory pretty much prevents sustainable success, as fate determines where the wheel will stop on the next spin.

GOAL THEORY

Most researchers argue that having SMART (specific, measurable, achievable, relevant, time-bound) goals to enhance specific resources is necessary for success. However, Richard St. John in his book *The 8 Traits Successful People Have in Common* argues that goals are *not* essential for achieving success. I was never able to ascertain his thinking why not!

INTENTION THEORY

In his book *Three Simple Steps*, Trevor Blake argues that "intentions" is a better term for goals. An intention has been defined as an "idea that you plan (or intend) to carry out. If you mean something, it's an intention. Your goal, purpose, or aim is your intention. It's something you mean to do, whether you pull it off or not." While it may be merely semantics, I really like the idea of having "intentions" rather than "goals."

PREVIOUS SUCCESS(ES) THEORY

There is scientific evidence that previous success with achieving goals (intensions, promises, desires) contributes to future success. Many researchers embrace the age-old adage that "success breeds success." While the phrase has been spoken by numerous people over many centuries, Mariel Margaret Hamm-Garciaparra (Mia Hamm), the two-time Olympic gold medalist soccer icon, is often credited with originating it. In sports, this theory is quite widespread because it does seem to work. While it seems reasonable that a first success (win) would naturally lead to more successes, this theory does not explain how to get the initial success (win). A recent study found that *greater amounts of initial success failed to produce greater subsequent success.*

INITIAL MOMENTUM THEORY

Albert-László Barabási, in his book *The Formula*, found that initial momentum is essential for success and that: (1) it doesn't matter who offers the initial support; (2) the more initial support the more success is virtually guaranteed; and (3) repeated interventions yield decreasing returns. It should be noted that "some" initial support leads to success, but a "lot" doesn't increase the amount of success.

FAILURE-PERSISTENCE THEORY

There exists empirical evidence that failure on goals (intentions or promises) often leads to eventual success. *Persistent* failure means any two or more failures by a person in any rolling period of twelve months and is defined as "a person's predisposition to persist with the effort to achieve a selected goal, finding the personal resources to overcome the obstacles, fatigue, stress, and other distractors."[8] Persistence after failure is strongly influenced by the perceived cause of the failure. Research shows there are three kinds of failure: (1) preventable, (2) unavoidable/complexity-related, and (3) innovative or intelligent. I incorporate this theory into my new success model and utilize John Martin's *The Power of Persistence* as my main source of material.

"JUST-IN-TIME" (JIT) THEORY

This theory suggests that it is more advantageous to obtain the knowledge, skills, or resources as needed to accomplish one or a few specific goals (or intentions) rather than accumulating resources simply because you might need them later. Living with a mindset of scarcity results in all kinds of problems. "Just-in-Time" (JIT) Theory counters this mentality by focusing on what you can leverage in the present to address what's immediately in front of you.

---

8. Constantin, Ticu & Holman, Andrei & Hojbota, Ana-Maria. (2011). Development and Validation of a Motivational Persistence Scale. *Psihologija*. 45947. 99-120. 10.2298/PSI1202099C.

In biology, there is a theory (law) of use and disuse that states that an organ's size and function is determined by how much it is used (for example, muscles increase after exercise). If resources are not used, they weaken and deteriorate.

EXCHANGE THEORY

This theory proposes that success is the result of an exchange process—giving and receiving. Though somewhat mysterious and perhaps a bit "New Age," scientific research has shown that giving and receiving does appear to exhibit "energy." Something of value must be given up (or sacrificed or exchanged) for something else of value to achieve a goal (intention or promise), though the exchange doesn't have to be equal in value. It is true that you can have anything (achieve any goal, including becoming rich or famous) you want if you are willing to pay the price (which is not always money) and (ironically) if you help enough people get what they want!

Reciprocity also comes into play in exchange theory. For many years, my dear friend and I have been going out to lunch together. He pays for both of us one time and I the next time. This is how it should be, and we are very happy with this arrangement. However, some people are takers only! For instance, I have taken another friend to lunch and dinner many times. But he has never taken me. I understand he does this with other friends as well.

When there is a failure in reciprocity, the best course of action is not to "deal" with the non-reciprocating person in the future. Consider this version of an Aesop fable: A farmer was walking through his field one cold winter morning. On the ground lay a poisonous snake, stiff and frozen with the cold. The snake begged the farmer to pick it up and put it in his bosom to warm it back to life. When the snake recovered, it bit the farmer in the heart. As the farmer was dying, he said to the snake, "Why did you bite me?" The snake replied, "You knew what I was when you picked me up." The moral of this story is we "know" the people who aren't grateful and who will use us if we allow. If we stop dealing with them, they usually leave us alone and move on to other victims.

Nevertheless, one researcher said to give away something very precious to you and to give it to someone you don't particularly like. Only then can you get the complete benefit from giving. I like this idea, but I know it would be difficult to do. Giving and receiving are such critical factors in success that I incorporate both into my new formula.

THERMODYNAMICS THEORY

Similar to exchange theory, this theory holds that the total energy within a person stays the same. Energy cannot be created or destroyed—it can only be changed (exchanged) from one form into another. Remember, there can't be perpetual motion because the second law states that in an isolated system, entropy always increases. Entropy is the part of energy that cannot be put to work in some way. So, at some point a person runs out of energy (dies) unless he/she gets access to a new source (a miracle).

POWER-DEPENDENCE THEORY

Power-dependence theory describes how people rely on others for valued resources and determines the distribution of power in relationships. This theory implies that the more resources a person has, the more power he or she can command over others. Some researchers equate power with success, but there exists no scientific evidence. Nevertheless, there is considerable evidence that success is dependent on relationships with family, friends, mentors, networks, followers, etc. Napoleon Hill was one of the first success researchers to identify the importance of the help and cooperation of others. Hill conceived of the idea of a Mastermind—two or more people working toward a common goal can achieve more than working individually (synergy).

INTELLIGENCE THEORY

Empirical research has debunked the theory that success is always equal to intelligence and that IQ (as a trait) remains stable throughout life.[9] A high IQ, however, is still one (psychological) resource that is a moderate predictor of success in life. Nevertheless, it is common for people with superior intellect not to achieve success. Paula J. Caproni in her book *The Science of Success* writes "Although book smarts [IQ] may help us get high grades in school, this kind of intelligence isn't

---

9. Paula J. Caproni, *The Science of Success: What Researchers Know that You Should Know* (Van Rye Publishing, LLC, 2017), 6.

broad enough to help us succeed in a complex, ambiguous, and ever-changing world in which real problems are often hard to define, the one best answer doesn't always exist, and we need the support of others [sociology] to accomplish our goals."

MINDSET THEORY

In her book *Mindset: The New Psychology of Success*, Carol S. Dweck established the theory that people with a growth mindset believe that intelligence and abilities can be developed through effort, persistence, trying different strategies and learning from mistakes. Dweck presents a great deal of research to support her theory.

MEMETICS THEORY

Memes are "copied" (or imitated, selected, or taught) habits, skills, stories, ideas, behaviors, songs, or any kind of information passed from person to person. Meme theory emerged from the theory of Universal Darwinism. When any information is copied, "evolution" occurs just as biology evolves by the selection of genes. Memes evolve because people select varied information, combine, make copying errors, or intentionally alter ideas.

BEHAVIORAL THEORY

Because feelings, thoughts, intentions, or desires were for a long time considered "unscientific illusions" and could not be measured, behavioral theory involved only how people learn through their experiences and that our behavior is just a response to rewards and punishments.

LEARNING THEORY

This theory describes how people receive, process, and retain knowledge during learning. Researchers say there are five primary educational learning theories: behaviorism, cognitive, constructivism, humanism, and connectivism. Additional learning theories include transformative, social, and experiential.

INFORMATION PROCESSING THEORY

This theory focuses on how our brains sort out information that we receive and/or to which we pay attention, how it is encoded and stored in either our short-term or long-term memory. I like this theory for success. The analogy often used is that of a biological computer—the brain is the hardware (information processor), and the mind is the software. However, today there is more emphasis on the rest of our bodies and the interaction with the brain.

PLANNED BEHAVIOR THEORY

This theory, also called intention theory, suggests that intention (willingness) to perform a certain behavior will lead to a specific (positive) outcome. For example, if you *plan* to write an article or book, you start performing specific activities such as doing research on your topic and writing a draft.

HABIT THEORY

This theory proposes that behavior is attached to the circumstances in which it occurs because of a learned stimulus-response connection. Therefore, when the circumstance occurs, we automatically exhibit the behavior. After multiple stimulus-response episodes, the behavior becomes a habit. However, the 21-day habit rule, which says that if you do an activity for 21 days, it will become a habit, is a misinterpretation of what Maxwell Maltz wrote in his 1960 book *Psycho-Cybernetics*. According to Maltz, you will act like the sort of person you conceive yourself to be. Your nervous system cannot tell the difference between an *imagined* experience and a *real* experience.

LEAST ACTION/RESISTANCE THEORY

While studies conclude that "action" is required for personal success, proponents of the least action/resistance theory argue

THE BLIND MEN AND THE ELEPHANT | 73

that the quickest path is the one that requires the least effort and/or offers the least resistance. Mike Hernacki writes in his book *The Ultimate Secret to Getting Absolutely Everything You Want*, "When you become absolutely clear in your own mind that you are willing to do whatever it takes to achieve your goal, the mechanism—the *principle*—starts creating shortcuts for you. It starts eliminating the need to do certain items. It brings your goal to you with accelerating acceleration and without nearly all the trouble you thought was necessary." This theory suggests that the quickest route to anything (including success) is a straight line. Yet, many researchers have found that obstacles overcome (and failures learned from) actually enhance future success.

GENETIC THEORY

I am intrigued by the idea that some people are "born to succeed" and do so despite everything they do, or don't do. This theory suggests that success is mostly (or completely) in the DNA and even though some of these people have a string of failures, they are generally (overall) successful throughout life.

Joseph Maroon in his book, *Square One: A Simple Guide to a Balanced Life,* argues that epigenetics ("in addition to or above genetics") plays a key role in a person achieving success. Maroon states "genes, the distinct stretches of DNA (first identified in 1953), determine everything about us; our height, hair, eye and skin color, athleticism, how we respond to environmental triggers, and so much more. Since genes are the molecular units of heredity passed from parent to offspring, our genes were considered our destiny—the concept of 'genetic determinism.'"

However, Maroon notes, "We now know that only about 30 percent of our genetic code falls into the 'determined' category, which means the remaining 70 percent is actually under our control...in short, it is possible to flip 'switches' on or off in roughly 70 percent of our genes, either for a more positive result or to our detriment."

Richard St. John argues in *The 8 Traits Successful People Have in Common* that "there is a myth that success is inherited, passed down from parent to child, but my [St. John] research shows it's not true. I [St. John] have interviewed many successful people's children and, yes, some achieved success themselves, but it was not due to genetics. It was because they watched their parents doing the things that lead to success, copied them, and slowly developed the eight success traits themselves." St. John maintains that "the eight traits are *not* genetic traits. Successful people aren't born with them; they develop them by taking action." In other words, "Successful people don't inherit them (the eight traits), or sit around thinking about them, they do them."

Genetic theory is analogous to the predestination theory in religion, the "great man" theory in leadership, and the "set-point" theory in happiness. Researchers argue that success is not actually in the DNA but is a "gift" of God (or the gods or aliens or some other supreme being/entity) bestowed upon deserving individuals. For example, Florence Scovel Shinn (1925) in her little book, *The Game of Life & How to Play It* hints at "predestination theory" when she states, "There is a place that you are to fill and no one else can fill, something you are to do, which no one else can do" (p. 9). While I was writing this book (December 2022), the world population exceeded 8 billion people, and it was estimated that approximately 117 billion people had ever lived on Earth. It boggles the mind to consider that each of these human beings have or had a specific purpose for having been born. The Georgia Guidestones contained the recommendation to maintain the world's population at under 500 million! This could be quite impossible as what would become of the other 7.5 billion people already living? Remember there are over 340 million people living in the US as of 2024.

DOUBLE PREDESTINATION THEORY

This theory holds that God dictated that some people are predestined to go to heaven (success) while others are foreordained to go to hell (failure). For universalism predestination theory, God has chosen all to receive salvation. Extreme Pelagianism theory holds that God has given humankind laws and commandments and freedom to choose (think choice theory) to obey those rules and if so, God saves them. Semi-Pelagianism theory grants that salvation is by grace but holds that people have the freedom to accept or decline this divine gift.

THE "GREAT MAN" OR "GREAT PERSON" THEORY

This theory implies that leaders are born with inherited traits that endow them for success (i.e., power, authority, prestige, and position). Further, the theory states that these DNA-encoded characteristics remain stable over time and that these leaders are destined to fulfill the roles.

SET-POINT THEORY

Martin Seligman developed a simple formula (only three variables) for measuring happiness. It was $H = .50S + .10C + .40V$, where (H) stands for happiness and is equal to the sum of (S) one's genetic set-range for happiness, (C) their life circumstances, and (V) factors under their voluntary control. Moreover, Seligman's research suggests that people are born with (or very quickly develop) a "set point" for determining a constant level of happiness throughout life. It has been argued that the set-point theory of happiness suggests that levels of subjective well-being are determined primarily by heredity and by personality traits ingrained early in life and remain relatively constant throughout people's lives. For instance, studies show that while happiness for lottery winners increases initially, the winners' happiness after a few months or so returns to the level before they won.

Seligman's research shows that circumstances (in particular, wealth) play a less important role in our happiness than most of us believe. For example, executives report only slightly higher levels of happiness than ordinary people. Research also shows that people who become paraplegic eventually return to their previous levels of happiness.

The logic is if there is a set-point for happiness, there might be one for success. It is interesting to note that many people have achieved success, lost it, regained success, perhaps lost it again, then become successful an additional time or multiple succeeding times. Could this be a return to a person's set-point for success? Or is success simply a matter of being happy, being a game, expecting or a choice?

HAPPINESS THEORY

Sonja Lyubomirsky and colleagues in the book *The How of Happiness* argues that while 50 percent of Seligman's formula for measuring happiness ($\mathbf{H = .50S + .10C + .40V}$) is genetic (no control—but if Maroon is right, you actually may have a significant amount of control) and 10 percent life circumstances (little control), there is still 40 percent in which a person has a great deal of control (the voluntary factors). So, perhaps success is similar to happiness in that it has a genetic or set-point component—perhaps even a significant part.

Lyubomirsky identified 12 "Happiness Activities" that a person could do (voluntarily) that were scientifically proven to enhance their personal happiness:

1. Express gratitude

2. Cultivate optimism

3. Avoid overthinking

4. Practice acts of kindness

5. Nurture social relationships

6. Develop strategies for coping

7. Learn to forgive

8. Increase "flow" experiences

9. Savor life's joys

10. Commit to goals

11. Practice religion and spirituality

12. Take care of your body

Ironically, these 12 activities are highly correlated with becoming an authentically successful person, and I integrated them into my success formula. These 12 can be categorized into physiology, one; psychology, three; sociology, four; and philosophy, two. Two of the twelve activities will fit all four sides of my pyramid model, (8) increase "flow" experiences and (10) commit to goals.

So, which comes first—success or happiness? I originally thought a person had to be successful before he/she could be happy. However, a review of 225 studies in the *Psychological Bulletin* found that happiness doesn't necessarily follow success. In fact, it's just the opposite—happiness leads to success. According to the study's findings, happy people seek out and undertake new goals that reinforce their happiness and other positive emotions. Other factors also contribute to success, including intelligence, fitness, social support, and expertise. These include one physiology, fitness; two psychology, intelligence and expertise; and one sociology, social support.

GAME THEORY

While not technically "game theory," Florence Scovel Shinn writes in her book *The Game of Life & How to Play It*, "Most people consider life a battle, but it is not a battle, it is a game...of *Giving* and *Receiving*." Shinn also writes, "This means that whatever man [a person] sends out in word or deed [good or bad] will return to him [or her]." This is a most compelling theory in that "you reap what you sow." It suggests that *future consequences are predictably shaped by present actions*.

Actions are an important component of most success theories, including mine. In Deepak Chopra's book *The Seven Spiritual Laws of Success*, he devotes an entire chapter to "The Law of Giving." Chopra said essentially the same thing as Shinn did nearly 70 years earlier. Chopra writes, "You must give and receive in order to keep wealth and affluence—or anything you want in life—circulating in your life." Chopra used as an example the "seed" and said, "The seed must not be hoarded; it must give its intelligence to the fertile ground." Further, Chopra wrote, "The more you give, the more you receive…anything that is of value in life only multiplies when it is given… the easiest way to get what you want is to help others get what they want." Finally, Chopra writes, "the most powerful forms of giving are non-material. The gifts of caring, attention, affection, appreciation, and love are some of the most precious gifts you can give, and they don't cost you anything."

EXPECTANCY THEORY

This theory suggests that a person is motivated to perform if they know that their extra performance is recognized and rewarded. Success is an outcome of how much an individual wants a reward (valence), the assessment that the likelihood that the effort will lead to expected performance (expectancy) and the belief that the performance will lead to reward (instrumentality).

CHOICE THEORY

This is a popular theory among many of the world's current success researchers—success is a choice (also the title of a 1997 book by Rick Pitino). Developed by psychiatrist William Glasser in 1965, Choice Theory® states humans are motivated by a never-ending quest to satisfy five basic needs woven into our genes: (1) to love and belong, (2) to be powerful, (3) to be free, (4) to have fun, and (5) to survive. Many researchers, including Deepak Chopra, argue that "You must become consciously aware that your future is generated by the choices you are making in every moment of your life." Further, Chopra writes, "Whenever I make a choice, I will ask myself two questions: 'What are the consequences of this choice that I'm making?' and 'Will this choice bring fulfillment and happiness to me and also to those who are affected by this choice?'"

Glasser argues that successful people have the power to control only themselves and take responsibility for their own life through the choices they make. Moreover, they have very little power to control others and do not attempt to do so. Glasser writes, "Choice theory explains that, for all practical purposes, we choose *everything* we do, including the misery we feel [and the success we achieve]. Other people can neither make us miserable nor make us happy. All we can get from them or give to them is information. But by itself, information cannot make us do or feel anything. It goes into our brains, where we process it and then decide what to do."

ESOTERIC THEORIES

I considered other theories of success which I termed "esoteric." While these theories were often compelling, they did not have sufficient empirical support to be viable science of success theories. These included:

Law of Attraction Theory

Popularized by Rhonda Byrne in her 35 million-plus bestselling book *The Secret*, this is the idea that "positive thoughts bring positive results into a person's life, while negative thoughts bring negative outcomes. It is based on the belief that thoughts are a form of energy, and that positive energy attracts success in all areas of life, including health, finances, and relationships." Wallace D. Wattles was one of the first writers to promote this ancient theory. "Law of attraction" theory was very popular with New Age success researchers. Positive thinking (Peale, 1952) and Positive Mental Attitude (Hill & Stone, 1959), though similar but with more scientific support, came later.

Human Vibrational Theory

This theory suggests that a person sends out thoughts, emotions, and wills as vibrations into the universe. Every thought or mental state has a corresponding rate and mode of vibration. The higher the vibration, the longer the effects are. The lower the vibration, the more potent the effects are in the short term. While this is a fascinating theory, there isn't enough evidence to support it being viable for success.

Accelerating Acceleration Theory

Mike Hernacki in his book *The Ultimate Secret to Getting Absolutely Everything You Want* proposes that success responds to the phenomenon of accelerating acceleration, in that "When things begin moving toward each other [law of attraction], they move at an ever-increasing rate." In other words, once momentum starts, what you want moves toward you more quickly. I love this idea, but there is no empirical evidence that it is true. Nevertheless, it is similar to initial momentum theory that does have empirical support and is a finding by Barabási.

Quantum Electrodynamics Theory

This theory is said to be the most successful theory in science. This is because the flow of invisible particles and the effects of an invisible force field can power everything. But I wonder if it can be used to explain and predict personal success.

Combination of Life Balance and Trait Theories

My original success model was a combination of the life balance theory, which included balancing four sciences— physiology, psychology, sociology, and philosophy—and trait theory—specific traits common and unique to the four sciences. Research confirms that both theories are important. Although this combination of two theories worked better than any formula utilizing either alone, it still did not account for a large percentage of people becoming successful. Therefore, it seemed necessary to enrich it with principles from additional theories.

The scientific findings from the theories in this chapter regarding the factors that lead to success include:

1. Success can be wealth, fame or power, but authentic, sustainable, true success is the pursuit of such things as good health (physiology), educational achievement and/or creative endeavors (psychology), having fulfilling relationships (sociology) or peace of mind (philosophy) or combinations.

2. Authentic success is being or becoming *balanced* especially on four dimensions – physiology (taking care of your body), psychology (taking care of your mind), sociology (taking care of your relationships) and philosophy (taking care of your relationship with a higher power).

3. Constantly working hard or engaging in *deliberate* practice and enjoying work can lead to "flow," "happy accidents," and continuous improvement.

4. Somebody does not have to lose for you to succeed. Game theory has shown that success does not have to be a zero-sum game, where one player must win and the other lose like in playing chess. In addition to win-lose, there are lose-lose and *win-win* strategies in life. It is possible for all parties to benefit simultaneously, even if one side benefits more than the other.

5. Success is easier when you have *concentrated* resources of time, money and/or other resources

that can be converted or exchanged. Even though we are severely depleting natural resources on this planet, resources can be created.

6. You do not have to compete for resources, although many people are motivated to succeed via competition. Success in achieving goals most often occurs during *collaboration* rather than competition. You cannot achieve authentic success without the help of others and the fastest way to become successful is, paradoxically, to help others become successful.

7. Having a high IQ, developing a growth mindset, being optimistic and positive, making good choices regarding goals, and expecting to be successful are strategies for success.

8. Getting initial support, nurturing family and other relationships, practicing reciprocity, doing acts of kindness, forgiving, giving and receiving (exchange), and expressing gratitude are strategies for success.

9. Taking some actions daily even if small in all four areas and being willing to do whatever it takes to achieve your goals are strategies for success. Successful people do what they sometimes don't want to do or what others won't do.

10. Not becoming complacent after success(es) and persisting after failure(s) and learning from and building on both are strategies for success.

These 10 insights gleaned from analyzing the various theories of success were remarkedly consistent with the definition of success developed in Chapter 1. However, there were eight new findings that could enhance the definition, revealed in the following (in *italics*):

> True, Authentic or Sustainable Success is the process (1) through *choices, simplicity, imagination,* a growth mindset, *"quiet time," hard but enjoyable work* or deliberate practice *that results in "flow," the* initial support, *help* and collaboration *of others and reciprocity,* and *love of self, mind, others, and a higher power* of (2) recognizing and seizing quality ideas/opportunities that are scalable, unique, needful, demanded, value priced, and that you are passionate about, (3) planning, *preparing,* and exchanging resources including *time, money, belief (faith),* physiological, psychological, sociological (emotional) and philosophical to (4) *position* an ambitious, holistic, *differentiated* and balanced array of focused, *challenging, visualized* and *value-added* "written" SMART goals, *intentions, promises,* burning desires/dreams or visions by (5) assuming risk(s), (6) overcoming *fears, challenges, stressors, weaknesses, negative thoughts,* failure(s),

displaying grit, being persistent and *persevering,* (7) be willing to do whatever is necessary by taking enthusiastic, *massive* (or numerous micro), *determined* actions that (8) enhance "happy accidents" and continuous improvement, (9) develop *disciplined habits including a healthy body, mind and soul,* (10) positively influence you and your target audiences' life-satisfaction, well-being, fun and happiness with win-win strategies, and (11) *with self-confidence, self-control, self-discipline, forgiveness, giving back* and doing acts of kindness, *practicing gratitude, and keeping a positive attitude without becoming complacent.*

My next step was to "map" the success process from the above "final" definition of success. Therefore,

SUCCESS =

(1) Burning Desire for something (authentic success would be your passion, purpose, calling, what gives you "flow," your true north; Write it down and look at and think about achieving the goal or goals every day—even many times during the day)

⇩

(2) Show "love" for this burning desire and everything and everyone connected with it (I know this sounds "mushy", but it is critical determinant of authentic success)

⇩

(3) List what it will take to achieve this "desire" (goal, intention, promise, dream), be willing to do whatever it takes, inventory your current resources (strengths, money, time, skills) and how you can leverage them to achieve this desire. If you don't have the resources, determine how you will acquire them? Borrow? Exchange?

⇩

(4) Believe that you can achieve this desire

⇩

(5) Break the "desire" (goal, intention, promise, dream) into "achievable" parts—be SMART about what must be done and in what order

⇩

(6) Work hard, do deliberate practice (do what others won't) and take actions daily (either

micro, medium or major) to achieve small wins or continuous progress (don't go to bed at night until have achieved something toward attaining your goal)

⇩

(7) Get initial support and remember every successful person had someone helping them

⇩

(8) Display grit, be persistent, turn failures into wins and wins into habits.

The theories discussed in this chapter are not the only ones that could explain and/or predict what causes some people to become successful and others to fail. Nevertheless, the most common theories were presented. While some, like the Law of Attraction theory, lacked scientific evidence, they were nonetheless compelling. In addition to the life balance and trait theories, research in this chapter revealed that there are nine theories that could scientifically contribute to a formula for success that could account for a larger percentage of people becoming successful.

For example, we now know that (1) luck or "happy accidents" which happen in the process of "taking action" in another area is involved even though early on I thought luck wasn't a factor, merely an excuse for an unidentified force. Further, we also know that (2) genetics or DNA plays a role in success though it may be a minor one. Moreover, we know that (3) resource management, (4) exchange, and (5) goal/intention theories are important though all were implied in my original pyramid model. Finally, research in this chapter has demonstrated that (6) choice, (7) expectancy, (8) least action/resistance, and (9) game theories play a role in authentic success attainment as well.

In sum, I'm going to add these additional theories to my original life balance/trait theory or formula, and doing so should result in a high percentage of people becoming successful. But first, let's do a deep dive into the life balance theory since it is one of the two pillars of my formula.

CHAPTER 3

SOME DAYS YOU EAT SALADS

Life Balance Theory Importance and Why It Alone Isn't Enough

Nido Qubein, the long-time and successful president of High Point University in North Carolina, in his book, *The Time is Now; The Person is You* (2005) writes, "To acquire balance means to achieve that happy medium between the minimum and the maximum that represents your optimum. The minimum is the least you can get by with. The maximum is the most you're capable of. The optimum is the amount or degree of anything that is most favorable toward the ends you desire." Moreover, Qubein writes, "Success is not a matter of luck, an accident of birth, or a reward for virtue. It is strictly a matter of decision, commitment, planning, preparation, and careful execution." In other words, success is balance!

When you have four variables or four sciences in my pyramid theory of success, mathematically it is better to be average (5 points out of 10) in all four (20 points) than to be great in one (perfect 10) and below average (3) in the other three (19 points). An element of my model is that a high score (even a "Perfect 10") on one component cannot compensate for low scores on one or more of the other three variables. Therefore, the balance score (2 to 10) is lowered when one or more of the scores for the four variables are higher or lower than a point. Even though we have known for a long time the importance of balance in our lives, researchers have not yet adequately defined the construct. Nevertheless, quite a few formulas and models, including mine and many others, have been developed to measure life balance and its relationship to personal success.

The remainder of the quote for the title of this chapter is: "Some days you eat salads and go to the gym, some days you eat cupcakes and refuse to put on pants, it's called balance." While I can identify with this quote, it's not the kind of balance being referred to regarding success. Life balance is the concept of managing the different segments of life with the goal of equilibrium and creating synergy.

I chose the pyramid shape since I knew the four sides needed to be as close to equal as possible because if one side was way out of balance, then the whole pyramid could collapse. Each of the four sciences have a score of 1 to 10 points with 10 being "perfect." Note: It was hardly possible to score a 1 or even a 2 on any side. For example, I had hypothesized that Physiology consisted of a minimum of physical attractiveness since research showed that good-looking people had an easier path to success, diet/nutrition, exercise, and sleep. So, someone reasonably handsome, in good physical condition who exercised regularly, got sufficient sleep/rest and proper nutrition would score a 7, 8 or 9.

My model was non-compensatory as it was better to score average (5 to 7) on all four areas than to be very high in one (9 or 10) and very low in another (3 or 4). This was because balance was what accounted for the greatest part of success. The balance score would be between 2 and 10 (perfectly balanced—all four sides the same number or within one point; 8 if one of the four was two points or more points below the next highest, 6 if two of the four were two or more points lower, etc.). That is why I decided to multiply the balance score by the sum of the four sciences.

MY ORIGINAL 1976 MODEL/THEORY

In my original 1976 Personal Marketing Pyramid model, the four sides of the pyramid—physiology (body), psychology (mind), sociology (emotions), and philosophy (soul)—require balance to maintain the integrity of the structure. Extending this, I determined that there were a set of distinctive "resources" associated with each of the four areas.

Physiology

- Nutrition/hydration
- Rest/sleep
- Exercise
- Clothing
- Grooming/cleanliness
- Posture
- Attractiveness

- Laughter/play/fun
- Stress management

Psychology

- Reading
- Education/knowledge
- Learning
- Games
- Laughter/play/fun

Sociology

- Relationships/putting others first
- Family
- Friends/companionship
- Coworkers/mentors
- Followers
- Organizations/membership/belonging

Philosophy

- Religion/faith/belief
- Prayer/meditation
- Ethics/morals/integrity
- Giving/charity/gratitude

Since creating the model/theory in 1976, I recognized that there were 11 synergies resulting from interaction effects between the life segments, so that two or more worked together to produce a combined effect greater than the sum of their separate effects. Below are some examples of how this works in practice.

Figure 3.1: Interaction Effects in My Original Model

This figure shows the interaction effects in my model/theory:

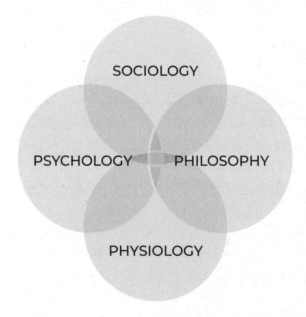

1. **Physiology and Psychology**
   Eating or exercising while studying a book

2. **Physiology and Sociology**
   Eating or exercising with a significant other (romantic partner/spouse, family member, friend, or mentor)

3. **Physiology and Philosophy**
   Meditating while resting, eating, or exercising

4. **Psychology and Sociology**
   Studying with a significant other (romantic partner/spouse, family member, friend, or mentor)

5. **Psychology and Philosophy**
   Reading and reflecting (psychology) about a philosophical issue (philosophy)

6. **Sociology and Philosophy**
   Attending church with a significant other (romantic partner/spouse, family member, friend, or mentor)

7. **Physiology, Psychology, and Sociology**
   Playing Dominos or a card game (psychology) while dining (physiology) with significant other (romantic partner/spouse, family member, friend, or mentor) or others (sociology)

8. **Physiology, Psychology, and Philosophy**
   Reflecting on a philosophical issue (philosophy) while dining (physiology) and reading (psychology)

9. **Physiology, Sociology, and Philosophy**
   Discussing a philosophical issue while dining
   with a significant other (romantic partner/spouse,
   family member, friend or mentor) or others

10. **Psychology, Sociology, and Philosophy**
    Discussing a philosophical issue with a significant
    other (romantic partner/spouse, family member,
    friend, or mentor) or others while playing a card
    game

11. **Interaction of All Four Sides**
    Discussing a philosophical issue while dining
    with a significant other (romantic partner/spouse,
    family member, friend, or mentor) or others and
    playing a card game

As can be seen from the four intersecting circles, there are 11 interaction effects in my model. There are six interaction effects between two of the four components: (1) Physiology and Psychology; (2) Psychology and Sociology; (3) Sociology and Philosophy; (4) Philosophy and Physiology; (5) Physiology and Sociology; and (6) Psychology and Philosophy. There are four interaction effects between three of the components: (7) Physiology, Psychology and Sociology; (8) Psychology, Sociology and Philosophy; (9) Sociology, Philosophy and Physiology; and (10) Philosophy, Physiology and Psychology. Finally, there is an interaction effect between all four sides; (11) Physiology, Psychology, Sociology, and Philosophy.

There are many combinations of actions that can be taken to meet the four categories of needs. Synergy begins when there is interaction between two or more of the sides of the pyramid resulting in the combined effect being greater than the sum of the parts. The model is holistic in that the parts of the pyramid are interconnected and can be explained only by reference to the whole. We should not view one side of the pyramid as separate from the other three. The pyramid is also non-compensatory in that elevated attention to one side cannot compensate for neglect of another side.

Unknown to me until 2024, Stephen R. Covey, A. Roger Merrill, and Rebecca R. Merrill had modeled this in their book *First Things First*. The authors call the spot where the four "needs" overlap—all four needs working at the same time—as "The Fire Within." I, on the other hand, was calling it the "Sweet Spot." The authors write, "These needs [physical, mental, social and spiritual] are real and deep and highly interrelated. Some of us recognize that we have these needs, but we tend to see them as separate 'compartments' of life. We think of 'balance' as running from one area to another fast enough to spend time in each one on a regular basis." They go on to write, "It's where these four needs overlap that we find true inner balance, deep fulfillment, and joy." The authors argue that we must see the *interrelatedness* and the powerful *synergy* of these four needs before our "work has meaning, relationships have depth and growth, health becomes a resource to accomplish worthwhile purposes."

Covey and his colleagues write that this 11th interaction effect or "The Fire Within" was the key to our "spiritual need to leave a legacy." It's transformative—"Food, money, health, education, and love become resources to reach out and help fill the unmet needs of others." This means living for a purpose higher than self.

Long before Covey, Merrill, and Merrill, and before the word "synergy" had even been coined, Napoleon Hill hinted at the concept of synergy. In Hill's later writings, he discussed the idea of "Cosmic Habit Force," a principle through which all the other principles of success reinforce each other and create a whole that is greater than the sum of its parts—the classic definition of synergy.

Hill also conceived the "Mastermind," a peer-to-peer mentoring group used to help members solve their problems with input and advice from the other group members. When synergy emerges between the individuals, their force increases exponentially, creating a "third mind." As he writes: "The coordination of knowledge and effort between two or more people who work towards a definite purpose in a spirit of harmony.... No two minds ever come together without creating a third, invisible, intangible force, which may be likened to a third mind (the Mastermind)."

In *If Life is a Game, These are the Rules,* Author Chérie Carter-Scott writes "The challenge of Rule One is to make peace with your body, so that it can effectively serve its purpose and share its valuable lessons of acceptance, self-esteem, respect, and pleasure." Regarding acceptance, Carter-Scott writes, "If any small part of you believes that you would be happier if you were thinner, taller, larger, firmer, blonder, stronger, or some other physical alteration you think would magically transform your life for the better, then you might want to spend some time learning about the value of true acceptance." She continues,

"There is much documented proof that the mind and body are connected, so acceptance of your body is not only essential for your emotional well-being, it is essential for your physical health, as well. Denying your body complete acceptance can lead to illness, whereas practicing acceptance can heal disease." She tells her clients and students, "Love all parts of yourself, and if you can't love them, change them. If you can't change them, then accept them as they are." Good advice.

DANFORTH'S MODEL

While I thought I had discovered something completely original in my pyramid of four sciences and balance model, I found out many years later that an author had already written about a similar model. The book *I Dare You!* published in 1931 by William H. Danforth, the founder of the Ralston-Purina Company, contains a model—four sides of a square—that is like my pyramid model and uses essentially the same four variables or factors. I'm certain I had not read this book in 1976 when I conceived of my four-sided pyramid-shaped model or theory after having read numerous biographies and autobiographies of successful people. However, Danforth's model/philosophy, which he called "four-square" living or the "four-fold" life, was very similar to mine and very similar to what students at Caney Creek Community Center, later Alice Lloyd College, had created between 1917–1923! Danforth maintained that to enjoy a successful life, individuals had to *balance* physical, mental, social, and "religious" needs.

Danforth argues that "Life cannot be complete unless we develop all four sides. Each side that is developed in turn stimulates the other three sides. 'All for one and one for all.' Life's Musketeers work together for one common end. All down the pages of history great lives have been telling us this secret of the four-fold life."

You may recall Aesop's tale of the four oxen and the lion:

> A lion used to prowl about a field in which four oxen used to dwell. Many a time he tried to attack them; but whenever he came near, they turned their tails to one another, so that whichever way he approached them he was met by the horns of one of them. At last, however, they began quarrelling among themselves, and each went off to pasture alone in a separate corner of the field. Then the lion attacked them one by one and soon made an end of all four. https://fablesofaesop.com/the-four-oxen-and-the-lion.html

So, like my model/theory, Danforth's incorporates synergy, though he didn't use that term specifically.

Danforth had the reader draw a square diagram of his/her life as he/she was living it to ascertain how near to "four-square" living the person was currently. Most people will have a lopsided square and can easily see which side or sides needs work.

One thing that Danforth did in addition to having the reader draw their current square was to also draw the "even-sided" four-square diagram and label it. Then, in the middle, Danforth had the person write "My Checker" and sign his/her initials. He did this, I think, so that people would have a "visual" to look at to commit to taking action on whichever side(s) that was/were not perfectly equal. Danforth states, "No plan is worth the paper it is printed on unless it starts you doing something [taking action]." For the remainder of the book, Danforth presents concrete or definite actions for each of the four sides of the square.

ALICE LLOYD COLLEGE'S MODEL

Before Danforth's 1931 model, there was a small college in the Appalachian Mountains of Eastern Kentucky, now named Alice Lloyd College, that used a model that contained the same items. See https://www.alc.edu/wp-content/uploads/2012/05/Purpose_Road_Diagram.jpg for the diagram. Research clearly shows that Alice Lloyd and June Buchanan were teaching this Purpose Road Philosophy as early as 1919 and definitely in the 1920s as the college's archives contain the original hand-drawn figure.

In the Alice Lloyd College model, there is a box/square labeled Responsibility. Inside this box/square is another box/square labeled "Self," which means a person is basically "good," but all people have a little "evil," But most interesting is the "Physical," "Mental," "Social" and "Spiritual" components. Recall Danforth labeled "Spiritual" as "Religious." From the Self extends Purpose Road, where "Conscience," "Duty," "Action," "Interest," "Courage," and Consecration" lead to

"World Service" and are circumscribed within an "Ocean of Power" and "Stream of Plenty" overseen by God.

In 2025, I re-visited Alice Lloyd College (ALC) and met with their president, Dr. James O. Stepp. ALC is one of a few "work" colleges still in existence in the US and charges NO tuition (like my alma mater, Berea College). Jim and I have known each other since around 2002 when I made my first gift to ALC. As I may have mentioned, I always start with a small donation to a new charity to "test" how they treat that gift. About that time, the State/Commonwealth had taken one of my rental houses for a road project. Since I didn't need the money from that sale and since much of it was capital gains, I decided to donate the proceeds. My Mother and I prayed where to give the money and even though we didn't have any specific connections to either the local university—University of Virginia's College at Wise (UVA-Wise) or ALC, we were led that I should donate to those schools. I personally delivered the checks to both UVA-Wise and ALC and told them they could do whatever they wanted with the endowments as long as they memorialized my father and honored my mother!

I don't know what Jim's title at ALC was at the time, but I was impressed with him. I have since learned that he has quietly raised over $80 million and that when he came to ALC he had only planned to stay one year to complete an internship. That was over 34 years ago! Jim's online biography states, "With humility and dedication (two very important components of authentic success) to the mission of the school, Dr. Stepp regards his time at Alice Lloyd College as part of a higher calling: 'It has been a great honor and privilege to be part of the greatest story ever told in higher education.'"

MEYER'S WHEEL OF LIFE MODEL

The literature doesn't seem to contain anything else after 1931 about utilizing life balance for achieving success until the 1960s, when Paul J. Meyer created his Wheel of Life model/theory soon after he started Success Motivation Institute®. This model features six evenly sliced pieces of pie that contribute to one's overall life balance: "Family and Home," "Financial and Career," "Mental and Educational," "Physical and Health," "Social and Cultural," and "Spiritual and Ethical." Myer included "Financial and Career" and "Family and Home"perhaps because even then the concept of work-life balance was in vogue.

Meyer's major contribution was to give people a helicopter view of what was working or not working in their lives.

I did a "wheel" for myself on March 16, 2022. For scoring, each of the six categories have a range of 0 to 10 (like my original pyramid model, but I didn't use 0). For Financial and Career, I gave myself an 8 because though I've been financially secure for a long time I was having a few problems at work. Also, I gave myself a self-score of 8 on Mental and Educational though I know as I'm getting older, I'm not as sharp as I used to be. The category Physical and Health had continued to decline in recent years and was then about a 4 (this was before my cancer diagnosis). For Social and Cultural, I rated myself a 7 even though during the pandemic I had not been visiting with friends in person. For Spiritual and Ethical, I rated as an 8 as I try very hard to live a Christian life. Note: research shows that any religion can assist you in becoming successful. Finally, for

Family and Home, I also rated as an 8. So, it was obvious that I needed to work on the Physical and Health piece of the pie/pizza/wheel even before cancer.

Now, do a "wheel" for yourself.

KIYOSAKI'S SUCCESS LIFE BALANCE MODEL

In 1973, *Rich Dad, Poor Dad* author Robert T. Kiyosaki was introduced to a success model at a seminar. He called this model (and the derivative model he formulated in 2001) a "learning tetrahedron." (A tetrahedron is a pyramid without the base—just four *equal* triangle sides.) The four sides in the original model were "Physical Intelligence," "Emotional Intelligence," "Spiritual Intelligence," and "Mental Intelligence."

Kiyosaki recounts learning about this diagram in *The Biggest Secret to My Success*:

> I'm often asked what I attribute to my success over the years, and as I reflect, I can point back to a weekend course [non-credit personal development] that changed my life...the instructor drew this simple diagram...on the flip chart with the words: physical intelligence, emotional intelligence, mental intelligence, and spiritual intelligence.... With the diagram complete, the instructor turned and said, "To develop into a

whole human being, we need mental, physical, emotional, and spiritual education."

Kiyosaki explains, "The reason physical intelligence is at the top of this diagram is because all learning is physical. For example, for a child learning to walk, the learning process relies on physical intelligence, more than mental intelligence. In school, learning to read, write, and do arithmetic is primarily a physical process. Like learning to walk, the student needs to do something." Having physical at the top violates the principle of balance for which Kiyosaki had advocated and that almost all researchers (even as far back as the early 1900s) say is paramount. If Kiyosaki's model is a true tetrahedron, then, by definition, there are four *equal* vertices. So, physical can't be at the top!

In 2001, Kiyosaki revised the model to position "Mental" as the vertex, with "Emotional," "Spiritual," and "Physical" forming the points of the triangular base.

Although focused on education and learning, this model comes the closest to my conceptualization of what constitutes success. Like me, Kiyosaki argues that "spiritual learning is not necessarily in the formal religious sense, although it can come from there also." In his 2015 book *8 Lessons in Military Leadership for Entrepreneurs,* Kiyosaki called these four items "cornerstones of discipline" and noted the holistic nature of the model. Further, Kiyosaki implies that if one or more of the cornerstones collapses, that people became "stuck in life."

SOME DAYS YOU EAT SALADS | 107

WAITLEY'S WHEEL OF FORTUNE MODEL

Denis Waitley, in his 1983 book *Seeds of Greatness*, envisions success as having eight equal slices of a pie that form a "Wheel of Fortune": "Mental," "Social," "Spiritual," "Physical," "Family," "Financial," "Professional," and "Community Support." I've been unable to determine why Waitley thought community support was so important.

COVEY'S FOUR DIMENSIONS MODEL

Covey developed a cyclical model along similar lines in 1989 that he titled the Four Dimensions of Renewal: "Physical," including "Exercise, Nutrition, Stress Management"; "Social/Emotional," including "Service, Empathy, Synergy, Intrinsic Security"; "Spiritual," including "Value Clarification & Commitment, Study & Meditation"; and "Mental," including "Reading, Visualizing, Planning, Writing."

Five years later, Stephen R. Covey, A. Roger Merrill, and Rebecca R. Merrill in their book *First Things First* wrote that "The essence of these needs [physical, social, mental, spiritual] is captured in the phrase 'to live, to love, to learn, to leave a legacy.' Each of these needs is vitally important. *Any one of these needs unmet, reduces quality of life.*" Further, the authors write, "Only as we see the interrelatedness and the powerful synergy of these four needs do we become empowered to fulfill them in a way that creates true inner balance."

Fifteen years after the publication of his *7 Habits* book, Covey in his 2004 book *The 8th Habit*, reconceptualized his theory with "Spiritual Intelligence" being in the middle, the core, and the most important component. "Mental Intelligence," "Physical Intelligence" and "Social Intelligence"—Covey again included "Emotional Intelligence" with "Social Intelligence"—surrounded "Spiritual Intelligence." Covey argued that spiritual intelligence "becomes the source of guidance of the other three." Because Covey was a man of deep faith, I can understand why he would hypothesize this approach.

George Sheehan, the running guru, describes four roles: being a good animal (physical), a good craftsman (mental), a good friend (social), and a saint (spiritual). He died four days short of his 75th birthday on November 1, 1993. He used to say humans come with a 75-year warranty, but it was not age with which he was concerned. It was life in the present. "Don't be concerned if running or exercise will add years to your life," he would say, "be concerned with adding life to your years."

There are two possible explanations for the similarities between all these models. The first is the "great-minds-think-alike theory," which states that the same theory/model evolves *independently* at different times. The other explanation is the "there-is nothing-new-under-the-sun theory," which states that early stories influence and/or become incorporated into newer stories. This is known as syncretism.

Most balance philosophies deal with these four constructs, whether called needs, dimensions, intelligences, sciences, values, or roles—it's all semantics. Regardless of the terminology (Danforth's "needs," my "sciences," or Covey's "dimensions" in 1989 or "intelligences" in 2004), all four of the components

SOME DAYS YOU EAT SALADS | 109

deal with all four parts of human nature: (1) body; (2) mind; (3) heart; and (4) spirit (soul) and originate in antiquity.

Interestingly, all four components have been alluded to in both the Old and New Testaments of the Bible. Three of these sciences are contained in one verse in Deuteronomy 6:5 (KJV): "And thou shalt love the Lord thy God with all thine *heart,* and with all thy *soul,* and with all thy *might.*" Only "mind" was left out. In the New Testament, Jesus adds "mind" but leaves out "might" (strength or body) in Matthew 22:37. However, two of the gospel writers (Mark & Luke) included all four. Mark 12:30 (NIV) reads, "Love the Lord your God with all your *heart* and with all your *soul* and with all your *mind* and with all your *strength.*" Luke 10:27 (NIV) was very similar, "Love the Lord your God with all your *heart* and with all your *soul* and with all your *strength* and with all your *mind....*"

MASLOW'S HUMAN NEEDS MODEL

Although not technically a life balance model, Maslow's (1943) Hierarchy of Needs explicitly contains three of the four components—physiological needs, psychological needs, and sociological needs, though Maslow termed sociological as "belongingness and love needs." I argue that Maslow's "self-actualization" could be classified as "spiritual."

Recent research suggests that Maslow never conceptualized his model as a pyramid or for it to be a hierarchy. Maslow always said that a lower-level need could be "worked on" simultaneously with a higher-level need. Ballard, Bridgman, and Cummings (2019) further assert:

> It's described as "Maslow's pyramid" when he did not create it and it's just not a good representation of Maslow's hierarchy of needs. It perpetuates unfair criticisms of the theory. For example, that people are only motivated to satisfy one need at a time, that a need must be 100% satisfied before a higher-level need kicks in, and that a satisfied need no longer affects behavior. Another is the view that everyone has the same needs arranged and activated in the same order. In his 1943 article in *Psychological Review*, Maslow anticipates these criticisms and says they would give a false impression of his theory. Maslow believed that people have partially satisfied needs and partially unsatisfied needs at the same time, that a lower-level need may be only partially met before a higher-level need emerges, and that the order in which needs emerge is not fixed.

PELLETIER'S CIRCLE OF LIFE MODEL

In his 1997 book *Permission to Win*, Ray Pelletier developed a life balance model that he called the Circle of Life. It consisted of 10 spokes on a wheel labeled (1) goals; (2) attitude; (3) educational; (4) family; (5) professional; (6) community/charity;

(7) financial; (8) spiritual; (9) leisure; and (10) physical fitness. Pelletier maintained that you come closest to a life of fulfillment where there is balance in all 10 areas.

RICHARDSON'S BALANCED "WHOLE LIFE" MODEL

In 1998, Cheryl Richardson, in her book *Take Time for Your Life,* proposed that there are six sides to a balanced, "whole" life. These included three that had been previously identified (1) emotional and physical health, (2) relationships, and (3) spiritual well-being. The emotional could be equivalent to mental. However, Richardson added three other variables (1) work, (2) fun and adventure, and (3) contributions to others which could be similar to relationships. Richardson showed what a typical "out of balance" circle looked like with work overwhelmingly dominating most people's life rather than spending time contributing to others, on their spiritual well-being or having fun.

KELLY'S LIFE BALANCE MODEL

In 1999, Matthew Kelly, in his book *The Rhythm of Life: Living Every Day with Passion & Purpose,* proposed that "there are four aspects to the human person: physical, emotional, intellectual, and spiritual" (p. 14). Like I did in 1976, Kelly calls for a balance in these four aspects of the human person. They all work together to make us a whole like my "holistic" approach.

This book was publicized as a guide to "help you to bring into focus who you are and why you are here." Further, Kelly stated, "Everything is a choice. This is life's greatest truth and its hardest lesson. It is a great truth because it reminds us of our power. Not power over others, but the power to be ourselves and to live the life we have imagined. It is a hard lesson because it causes us to realize that we have chosen the life we are living right now."

MATUSKA AND CHRISTIANSEN'S LIFE BALANCE MODEL

In 2009, Kathleen M. Matuska and Charles H. Christiansen published an article titled "A Proposed Model of Lifestyle Balance" in which they provide empirical evidence that "certain lifestyle configurations...lead to better health, higher levels of life satisfaction and general well-being." The article presents a proposed model of lifestyle balance involving five need-based occupational dimensions seen as necessary for well-being.

For Matsuka and Christiansen, what matters most for life balance is the relationship between activity configurations, environment, and associated life outcomes. In other words, individuals need congruence between activities, goals, and outcomes; and equivalence among four need-based dimensions in health, relationships, challenge, and identity. An overlap between the two ovals signifies they are necessary for a balanced life. Low congruence leads to an imbalanced life. Life balance is expected to relate to lower stress, higher need satisfactory, and higher personal well-being.

MCNEFF'S SEVEN SLICE PIE MODEL

In 2021, David J. McNeff published the book *The Work-Life Balance Myth,* which was touted as "an empowering guide that will show you how to shed the myth of the 'work-life balance' by merging the seven key components that make up your life to attain harmony and whole-life success." According to McNeff, "All of us have Seven Slices in our lives: our Family Slice, our Professional Slice, our Personal Slice, our Physical Slice, our Intellectual Slice, our Emotional Slice, and our Spiritual Slice. These all need to be served in some fashion—and in serving them, they, in turn, serve us."

One reviewer said, "This relatively simple but profoundly critical concept is at the heart of the method executive coach David McNeff has used to transform the lives and careers of his clients. It begins with two important facts: (1) stress happens—you can't avoid it; and (2) your existence is composed of far more than "work" and "life." The review goes on to say:

> Too often, we divide our lives into those two general categories, but we're all a lot more complex and our lives are richer than that. By being clear and mindful of all aspects of your life—the Seven Slices—you'll be more likely to find inner

harmony when stress impacts one of them. In *The Work-Life Balance Myth,* McNeff takes you on a deep dive into each of the Seven Slices, explaining the components of each Slice, signs that you may not be attending to each Slice in a healthy way, and hands-on methods for accessing an underserved Slice.

The Work-Life Balance Myth won't make your life perfect—no one can do that, and you shouldn't trust anyone who makes that promise. What this book will do is provide you with proven new ways of framing your life, seeing stress for what it is, and vastly improving your ability to navigate the emotional challenges that will inevitably arise in a way that serves your Seven Slices.

Trevor Blake, in his book *Three Simple Steps: A Map to Success in Business and Life* (2012), writes, "the path to financial independence went hand and glove with improvements in all aspects of a *balanced* life." While Blake didn't specify these "aspects," he appeared to be emphasizing synergy and balance in addition to his three steps. Blake continued, "We want to look back on our lives with a measure of pride that we achieved something worthwhile." I think by this statement Blake was hinting at "authentic" success. Finally, Blake writes, "There is never a wrong time to take control of your life."

In May 2022, Cambridge University Press published a book by one of my former Virginia Tech doctoral marketing professors, M. Joseph Sirgy titled, *The Balanced Life: Using Strategies*

SOME DAYS YOU EAT SALADS | 115

from Behavioral Sciences to Enhance Wellbeing. This is from Cambridge.org:

> The balanced life is a state of equally moderate-to-high levels of satisfaction in important and multiple life domains that contribute to overall life satisfaction. This book strives to improve the reader's understanding of what the balanced life is, and how it can be both achieved and maintained. Its primary goal is therefore to identify the major principles of life balance, and to introduce a comprehensive construct of the balanced life reflective of these principles. It discusses how life balance substantially contributes to subjective well-being—defined as life satisfaction, a preponderance of positive over negative feelings, and absence of ill-being—and explores strategies to attain life balance. It argues that achieving life balance, through manipulating one's thoughts and taking concrete action, will lead to increased personal happiness. Aimed at professional, academic, and lay audiences, this book is grounded in scientific studies related to work-life balance and the balanced life.

So, what is the optimal number of slices or sides for an effective life balance theory? As can be seen in Appendix C, six of 12 researchers found that four sides were best (Alice Lloyd College, Danforth, Caudill, Covey, Kelly, Kiyosaki). However, Maslow argued for five, while both Meyer & Richardson thought six sides were best. McNeff had seven, Waitley had eight, and Pelletier had 10 components in their models.

Recall that Linda and Richard Eyre in their 1997 book *Lifebalance: How to Simplify and Bring Harmony to Your Everyday Life* say, "The easiest number of areas to balance is *three*. It's relatively easy to juggle three balls, whereas four are many times more difficult." I initially considered just three—body, mind, and soul—but the research is clear: Nobody is a success without the help of a spouse, partner, family member, friend, mentor or significant other! Therefore, I think four slices—body, mind, soul, and social/emotions—are ideal.

While many researchers argue that to become successful, one must live a balanced life, all researchers and authors agree that there are several traits that all successful people have in common within the four areas of living a balanced life. Unfortunately, none of the researchers have determined the exact same traits! So, let's take a deep dive into trait theory since it is another large part of my new and improved success formula.

CHAPTER 4

IT'S ALL ABOUT THE TRAITS, MAN

Trait Theory Importance and Why It Alone Isn't Enough

There is much wisdom in the Native American parable that has been attributed to the Cherokee (or Lenape) people. It goes like this:

"I have a fight going on in me," the old man said. "It's taking place between two wolves. One has evil traits—he is anger, envy, sorrow, regret, greed, arrogance, self-pity, guilt, resentment, inferiority, lies, false pride, superiority, and ego."

The grandfather looked at the grandson and went on: "The other embodies positive traits. He is joy, peace, love, hope, serenity, humility, kindness, benevolence, empathy, generosity, truth, compassion, and faith. Both wolves are fighting to the death. The same fight is going on inside you and every other person, too."

The grandson took a moment to reflect on this. At last, he looked up at his grandfather and asked, "Which wolf will win?"

The old Cherokee gave a simple reply. "The one you feed."

Though the true origin of the story is unknown, there are numerous versions. Nevertheless, the parable suggests that a person has more control over "which wolf will win" than he or she may think. Some traits or resources, assets, strengths, talents, capabilities, abilities, competences, skills, behaviors, qualities, or virtues have been scientifically proven to be correlated with success. But like the life balance theory, which we have shown to be necessary for authentic success, traits—including those related to a positive mental attitude—are not sufficient alone to predict who will or won't become successful or to explain the success or failure of specific people.

In this chapter, I examine the various trait theories and categorize the traits into factors that could fit into one or more of the four sides of my life balance model—physiology, psychology, sociology, and philosophy. Note that the body-mind dilemma, which states that the more you have of one, the less you have of the other, is a myth. You can have equal parts of all four, including an identical number of traits in physiology/body and psychology/mind.

Trait theory, which is ascertaining the "traits" that successful people have in common, can be traced back to ancient times—for instance, Moses, the Buddha, Socrates, Plato, Aristotle. In ancient times, traits were considered virtues—a "trait of excellence, including traits that may be moral, social, or intellectual." For example, Moses had the Ten Commandments, which included not murdering, not stealing, not committing adultery, and not lying. Likewise, all Buddhists live by five moral precepts, four of which are like those contained in the Ten Commandments. Buddhism prohibits (1) the killing of living things, (2) taking what is not given, (3) sexual misconduct, (4) lying, and (5) using drugs or alcohol. It should be noted that the traits for success in any endeavor are the same, but perhaps with emphasis on specific traits for specific fields.

ARISTOTLE'S VIRTUES

Centuries after Moses and the Buddha, Aristotle, a student of Plato and a championship wrestler, developed a comprehensive list of virtues that when practiced would result in "living well." Several of the virtues on Aristotle's list were also taught by the Buddha: wisdom, kindness, patience, generosity, and compassion. The following is a content analysis of Aristotle's virtues in the context of my success pyramid:

Physiology

Temperance – Self-control and restraint

Psychology

Courage – Bravery and valor

Pride – Self-satisfaction

Good Temper – Equanimity, level-headedness

Wit – Sense of humor; the ability to embrace absurdity

Sociology

Liberality – Big-heartedness, kindness, charity, generosity

Honor – Respect, reverence, admiration

Friendliness – Conviviality and sociability

Friendship – Camaraderie and companionship

Philosophy

Magnificence – Radiance, joie de vivre (exuberant enjoyment of life)

Truthfulness – Straightforwardness, frankness, candor

Justice – Impartiality, evenhandedness, fairness

While most or all 12 virtues could fit into all four sides of my success pyramid in that you can be courageous spiritually or physically, it seemed more appropriate to fit each into a specific category. Temperance could be placed in Physiology because one should eat and drink in moderation and use self-control.

While not explicit in his 12 virtues, Aristotle did seem concerned about physiological virtues—health, exercise, rest. Indeed, Aristotle wrote quite a bit about exercise and physical fitness. He thought of exercise and fitness as both physiological and psychological. Moreover, Aristotle was one of the first people to suggest a mind-body relationship. So, Aristotle had a pretty good balance of virtues in each side of my original pyramid.

It should be noted that Wit (or sense of humor) was also contained in my Physiology side since laughter has a physiological effect. Also noteworthy, when I conducted a survey of undergraduate college students regarding the qualities of excellent professors, respect (Aristotle's Honor) and fairness (Aristotle's Justice) headed the list.

FRANKLIN'S VIRTUES

More than 2,000 years later, Benjamin Franklin, at the age of 20, developed his 13 Virtues. According to his book, *The Autobiography of Ben Franklin,* he practiced each for a week and after 13 weeks repeated the process. In a calendar year, Franklin was able to "work on" each virtue for four weeks (13 x 4 = 52). While it is unknown where Franklin got his list, only two explicitly matched Aristotle's 12 Virtues—temperance and justice.

The following is a content analysis of Ben Franklin's virtues in the context of my success pyramid:

Physiology

Temperance – "Eat not to dullness. Drink not to elevation."

Cleanliness – "Tolerate no uncleanness in body, clothes, or habitation."

Psychology

Resolution – "Resolve to perform what you ought. Perform without fail what you resolve."

Silence – "Speak not but what may benefit others or yourself. Avoid trifling conversation."

Industry – "Lose no time. Be always employed in something useful. Cut off all unnecessary actions."

Sincerity – "Use no hurtful deceit. Think innocently and justly; and if you speak, speak accordingly."

Sociology

Chastity – "Rarely use venery but for health or offspring; never to dullness, weakness, or the injury of your own or another's peace or reputation."

Justice – "Wrong none by doing injuries or omitting the benefits that are your duty."

Philosophy

Order – "Let all your things have their places. Let each part of your business have its time."

Frugality – "Make no expense but to do good to others or yourself," i.e., waste nothing.

Moderation – "Avoid extremes. Forbear resenting injuries so much as you think they deserve."

Tranquility – "Be not disturbed at trifles, or at accidents common or unavoidable."

Humility – "Imitate Jesus and Socrates"

As with Aristotle, Franklin's virtues or traits could apply to more than one side of my success pyramid. Three of Franklin's virtues would fit in all four sides: resolution (determination); industry (wise use of the resource "time"); and moderation (self-control, temperance, restraint).

Franklin's virtue of "silence" seems to be very similar to Trevor Blake's "quiet time" or getting out in nature for which he advocates in his 2012 book *Three Simple Steps: A Map to Success in Business and Life*. It could also be considered "meditation" and could fit in the philosophy side of my pyramid. Franklin's "chastity" might be like what Napoleon Hill (1937) in his book *Think and Grow Rich* referred to as "sex transmutation." Hill defined this as "the switching of the mind from thoughts of physical [sexual] expression to thoughts of some other nature. The sex desire is the most powerful of human desires. When driven by this desire, men [people] develop keenness of imagination, courage, willpower, persistence, and creative ability unknown to them at other times." As can be seen, there is a lot of interaction between the four sides of the pyramid.

SELIGMAN'S CHARACTER STRENGTHS

In 2002, Martin Seligman identified 24 character strengths, which he divided into 24 character strengths that lead to happiness (and perhaps success). The following is a content analysis of Martin Seligman's six classes of virtues (traits) in the context of my success pyramid:

Physiology

Zest – "Approaching all things in life with energy and excitement."

Psychology

Creativity – "Thinking of new ways to do things."

Curiosity – "Taking an interest in a wide variety of topics."

Open-Mindedness – "Examining things from all sides; thinking things through."

Love of Learning – "Mastering new topics, skills, and bodies of research."

Perspective – "Being able to provide wise counsel to others; looking at the world in a way that makes sense."

Honesty – "Speaking the truth; being authentic and genuine."

Bravery – "Embracing challenges, difficulties, or pain; not shrinking from threat."

Persistence – "Finishing things once they are started."

Self-Regulation – "Being disciplined; controlling one's appetites and emotions."

Sociology

Kindness – "Doing favors and good deeds."

Love – "Valuing close relations with others."

Social Intelligence – "Being aware of other people's motives and feelings."

Fairness – "Treating all people the same."

Leadership – "Organizing group activities and making sure they happen."

Teamwork – "Working well with others as a group or team."

Humor – "Making other people smile and laugh; enjoying jokes."

Philosophy

Forgiveness – "Forgiving others who have wronged them."

Modesty – "Letting one's successes and accomplishments stand on their own."

Prudence – "Avoiding doing things they might regret; making good choices."

Appreciation of Beauty – "Noticing and appreciating beauty and excellence in everything."

Gratitude – "Being thankful for the good things; taking time to express thanks."

Hope – "Expecting the best; working to make it happen; believing good things are possible."

Religiousness – "Having a solid belief about a higher purpose and meaning of life."

LYUBOMIRSKY'S HAPPINESS ACTIVITIES

Five years after Seligman debuted his list, Lyubomirsky identified 12 "happiness activities" that a person could voluntarily do that were scientifically proven to enhance their personal happiness. See the following for a content analysis of Lyubormisky's happiness activities (traits) in the context of my success pyramid:

Physiology

- Take care of your body.

Psychology

- Cultivate optimism.
- Avoid overthinking.
- Develop strategies for coping.
- Increase "flow" experiences.
- Commit to goals.

Sociology

- Practice acts of kindness.
- Nurture social relationships.
- Learn to forgive.

Philosophy

- Express gratitude.
- Savor life's joys.

While both Seligman and Lyubomirsky dealt with happiness traits, their lists were quite diverse. Only four, or one-third, of Lyubomirsky's 12 activities were a direct match—kindness, forgiveness, gratitude, and religiousness. Five, or 42 percent, of Lyubomirsky's 12 activities were not on Seligman's list of 24 virtues—avoid overthinking, develop strategies for coping, increase "flow" experiences, savor life's joys, and commit to goals. An additional three were what I'm calling "maybe matches"—Lyubomirsky's "cultivate optimism" might be similar to Seligman's "hope" in his Transcendence class, "nurture social relationships" might be similar to "social intelligence" in Seligman's Humanity class, and "take care of your body" might be similar to "zest" in Seligman's Courage class.

HILL'S SUCCESS PRINCIPLES

Trait theory didn't become a favorite technique of success researchers until nearly 200 years after Franklin, when Napoleon Hill published the book *Law of Success* (1928). Hill is said to have conducted actual interviews with hundreds of "successful" people and failures. Additional researchers have done the same kind of studies.

However, like Seligman and Lyubomirsky with happiness, these researchers didn't always agree which traits were most important even when using similar methodologies. All utilized frequency distributions, which are the least robust of all statistical analyses, to determine traits most associated with success. Hardly any of these researchers went beyond just counting the number of times a successful person mentioned a trait. The studies would have been much more scientific if there had been at least some rudimentary statistics performed on the data.

Hill, who is considered the father of the personal success genre of literature, claimed that his original 15 success principles—really, 16 with the "Mastermind" since it was discussed in the Introduction and in Hill's 1930 book, *Magic Ladder to Success;* many years later, 17 with the "Cosmic Habit Force" principle—were the result of his personally interviewing 500 successful people and thousands of failures over a 20-year time span! However, Hill claimed that the completed questionnaires were destroyed in a fire. In Hill's writings, however, he did not provide any (1) frequency distributions, such as 90 percent of the successful people interviewed said this or that; or (2) direct quotes from the questionnaires from people still living at the time he published the information.

Hill writes in the Author's Acknowledgment from the *Law of Success* (1928). [My notes are within brackets]:

> This course [book] is the result of careful analysis of the lifework of over one hundred men and women who have achieved unusual success in their respective callings. [Note: Hill does not specify exactly how he analyzed their lifework. It could have been from only newspaper clippings

and other published information as some researchers suggest.]

I have spent more than twenty years in gathering, classifying, testing, and organizing the lessons upon which the course [book] is based. In this labor I have received valuable assistance either in person or by studying the lifework of the following: [Hill lists 45 "famous" men.]

Of the people named, perhaps Henry Ford and Andrew Carnegie should be acknowledged as having contributed most toward the building of this course [book], for the reason that it was Andrew Carnegie [died in 1919] who first suggested the writing of the course and Henry Ford whose lifework supplied much of the material out of which the course was developed. [Note: Hill does not explicitly say that he actually met and/or personally interacted with Carnegie or Ford.]

I have studied the majority of these people at close range, *in person*. With many of them I enjoy, or did enjoy before their death, the privilege of close personal friendship which enabled me to gather from their philosophy facts that would not have available under other conditions. [Note: Hill does not specify which of the 45 men were "close personal" friends.]

With the exception of the psychological law referred to in Lesson One as the Mastermind, *I don't claim to have created anything basically new in this course* [book]. What I have done, however, has been to organize old truths and known laws into practical, usable form.

But what Hill did do was brilliant in that he, perhaps accidently, discovered many traits associated with successful people, including the Mastermind. Hill defined the Mastermind as the "coordination of knowledge and effort, in a spirit of harmony, between two or more people, for the attainment of a definite purpose." This is like what is today called networking—the action or process of interacting with others to exchange information and develop professional or social contacts. It is also similar to the definition of teamwork—a group of interdependent individuals who work together toward a common goal.

My research has revealed that regardless of where Hill got his principles of success, whether by primary research—personal interviews or questionnaires—with actual successful people, or by reading books and articles about them, or a combination, Hill made a significant contribution to the "science of success" literature simply by "organizing" the principles apparently from numerous sources—many of which have over the past 90 plus years been proven scientifically correct.

For example, I have a copy of a letter from Napoleon Hill to Charles Haanel in which he states, "I believe I ought to inform you that my present success and the success which has followed my work...is due largely to the principles laid down in the Master-Key System" (a book Haanel published in 1912).

Overall, there is not much of a balance of Hill's traits in the four sides of my pyramid model as Hill's traits are over one-half psychological.

CONTENT ANALYSIS OF HILL'S *LAW OF SUCCESS* AND *MAGIC LADDER TO SUCCESS* BOOKS

The following is a content analysis of Napoleon Hill's original success principles or traits from his *Law of Success* and *Magic Ladder to Success* books in the context of my success pyramid:

Physiology

(no traits for this side of the pyramid)

Psychology

- A Definite Chief Aim (Goal)
- Self-Confidence
- The Habit of Saving
- Imagination
- Enthusiasm
- Self-Control
- The Habit of Doing More than Paid For
- A Pleasing Personality

- Accurate Thinking
- Concentration
- Profiting by Failure
- Cosmic Habit Force (Habits) – Hill's definition of Cosmit Habit Force is voluntary habits becoming permanent through thinking

Sociology

- Initiative & Leadership
- Cooperation
- Tolerance
- The Mastermind – The Mastermind was not listed specifically as one of the traits but was part of the Introduction to the first edition in 1928 and later made a separate principle unto itself in 1930. Note that Cooperation was on these original lists which could be analogous to The Mastermind!

Philosophy

- Practicing the Golden Rule

Hill had temperance, self-control, and restraint as traits of successful people. So did Aristotle, Franklin, and Seligman. Since self-control is important physiologically (i.e., eating or drinking too much or too little), psychologically, sociologically, and philosophically, I have chosen to add this trait to all sides of my pyramid component of my new success formula.

In 1937 during the Depression, Napoleon Hill and his third wife Rosa Lee created something special in *Think and Grow Rich*. Hill was one of the first success authors to utilize a quasi-scientific approach to answering the question, "What causes a person to become successful?" Hill actually created a philosophy of success by integrating (he called it "organizing") the thinking and writings of many people.

In addition to "organizing" the existing literature (which apparently hadn't been done before), Hill (1937) maintained that he interviewed over 500 successful people and thousands of failures (conducted over 20 years, from 1908 to 1928). While obviously much hard work by both Hill and his wife was involved in producing the new 1937 manuscript, the book was mostly another version of Hill's *Magic Ladder to Success*, published in 1930, which itself was a condensed version of his *Law of Success* book published in 1928.

CONTENT ANALYSIS OF HILL'S *THINK AND GROW RICH* BOOK

The following is a content analysis of Napoleon Hill's principles (traits) from his book *Think and Grow Rich* in the context of my success pyramid:

Physiology

(no traits for this side of the pyramid)

Psychology

Desire – same as Definite Chief Aim (Goal)

Faith in Your Ability – same as Self-confidence

Autosuggestion – same as Concentration

Specialized Knowledge – no direct equivalent to a principle in *Law of Success*

Imagination – same as Imagination

Decision – no direct equivalent to a principle in *Law of Success*

Persistence – same as Profiting by Failure

Sexuality: Charisma & Creativity – no direct equivalent to a principle in *Law of Success*

The Subconscious Mind – similar to Accurate Thinking

The Brain – similar to Accurate Thinking

The Sixth Sense – Hill admits that this is "that portion of the subconscious mind which has been referred to as the creative imagination." However, this 13th principle (or step) gets a little more bizarre as he discusses his imaginary council meetings with a group he calls his "Invisible Counselors."

Sociology

Organized Planning – similar to Initiative & Leadership

Power of the Mastermind – same as Mastermind

Philosophy

Ten of the 13 principles from *Think and Grow Rich* were essentially the same or very similar to principles from his previous books *Law of Success* and *Magic Ladder to Success*, with eight renamed and the order of several rearranged. Note: Hill (and Rosa Lee) retained only two principles exactly: "Imagination" and "The Mastermind." However, three principles in *Think and Grow Rich* were new or a complete reworking of principles from Hill's previous books: "sexuality: charisma and creativity"; "specialized knowledge"; and "decision."

Traits Not Included in *Think and Grow Rich*

- The Habit of Saving
- Enthusiasm
- Self-Control
- The Habit of Doing More than Paid For
- A Pleasing Personality
- Cosmic Habit Force (Habits)
- Cooperation
- Tolerance
- Practicing the Golden Rule

Overall, however, the changes were mainly semantics! There wasn't a lot of difference between the 1928 *Law of Success* and

1930 *Magic Ladder to Success* books. Both books contained exactly the same "chapters" but with "The Mastermind" as being Lesson 1 and the other "traits" being moved down one place and "Lesson 17, The Habit of Health" being added in *Magic Ladder to Success.*

To view a comparison of Hill's principles or traits from his first three books showing how his thinking evolved over nine years, go to the book's website at https://thesuccesspyramid .com/

It is interesting to note that if the 15 to 17 "original" traits were scientifically derived, one would not have expected them to change so dramatically in nine years with the publication of *Think and Grow Rich.* The traits that were left out of *Think and Grow Rich* were (1) the habit of saving, (2) self-control, (3) the habit of doing more than paid for, (4) a pleasing personality, (5) tolerance, (6) practicing the Golden Rule, and (7) cosmic habit force. These were significant omissions as, for instance, the habit of saving means more financial resources would be available to achieve future goals.

The reason for the striking difference between the first two Hill books and *Think and Grow Rich* could be that Hill's third wife, Rosa Lee, was added as a "silent" author. Some researchers say Rosa Lee was in essence Hill's first "real" editor and should have been credited with a co-authorship (she in fact owned the copyright). Rosa Lee later published a book titled *How to Attract Men and Money* (1940). There are two "versions" of the remaining title (1) *How to Attract Men and Money: An Intimate Revelation for Women Past Eighteen* and *How to Attract Men and Money: How to Marry the Right Man and Help Your Husband Make a Fortune.* The subtitle was: *With Some Facts*

Men Ought to Know—Especially Those Who Wish to Stage a Comeback After Experiencing Defeat. Research suggests that Rosa Lee "brought Hill back from defeat!"

MCCOY'S "MEGATRAITS"

Though many researchers doubt that Hill administered actual questionnaires, there is considerable evidence that Doris Lee McCoy traveled all over the country and interviewed over 1,000 successful people during a one-year time span to ascertain her 12 success traits for her book *MegaTraits: 12 Traits of Successful People* (1988). McCoy's work has a lot of validity because (1) the people she claimed to interview were still living when her book was published, and (2) she quotes the respondents "directly."

While I'm not certain of her methodology, it appears it was a frequency distribution (i.e., counting how many times successful people credited a specific trait for their success). The following is a content analysis of Doris Lee McCoy's traits in the context of my success pyramid:

Physiology

"They're healthy, have high energy levels, and schedule time to renew themselves."

Psychology

"They enjoy their work."

"They have a positive attitude and plenty of confidence."

"They use negative experiences to discover their strengths."

"They're decisive, disciplined goal setters."

"They're persistent."

"They take risks."

"They've developed good communication skills and problem-solving skills."

Sociology

"They have integrity and help others succeed."

"They surround themselves with competent, responsible, and supportive people."

Philosophy

"They believe in a higher power, or, sometimes, just plain luck."

"They have a sense of purpose and a desire to contribute to society."

Like Hill, McCoy's traits lend heavily to the psychological—enjoying work, positive attitude, high level of confidence, use negative experiences, goal setters, persistent, risk takers with good communication and problem-solving skills. For sociology, McCoy found that successful people (I think she was an early advocate of authentic success) have integrity, help others succeed, and surround themselves with competent, responsible, and supportive people (teams, networks, mentors). Finally, for philosophy, McCoy found that successful people believe in a higher power (or luck), have a sense of purpose and desire to contribute to society.

ST. JOHN'S TRAITS

Twenty-two years after McCoy's work, St. John published *The 8 Traits Successful People Have in Common: 8 to be Great*. St. John spent 10 years interviewing over 500 people, including Bill Gates, Martha Stewart, and Richard Branson, collecting success stories, and analyzing millions of words.

There is also an abundance of evidence that St. John did interview the people he writes about. St. John found successful people to have eight key traits, as you will see in the below analysis. Like McCoy's list, St. John's list was heavily influenced by the psychology component—seven of the eight (or about 88 percent), with only one sociology.

Physiology

(no traits for this side of the pyramid)

Psychology

"Successful people are passionate about what they do."
"Successful people work hard while having fun."

140 | THE SUCCESS PYRAMID

"Successful people have a specific focus."

"Successful people push themselves out of their comfort zones."

"Successful people consistently come up with new ideas."

"Successful people are constantly getting better."

"Successful people are persistent through failure."

Sociology

"Successful people provide value to others."

Philosophy

As can be seen, the three lists are different. However, it seems to be mostly semantics. If these researchers were measuring the same thing, one wonders why there were *not* more of the traits the same from all three studies. However, using content analysis, one can see there are several similar traits though expressed in different words. Of course, the concept success could have meant something quite different in 1928, 1988, and 2010. But should there have been that much difference?

In addition to content analysis, another way to investigate if similar concepts exist is to use a technique called meta-analysis. A meta-analysis is drawing conclusions about a subject by examining the work of multiple independent researchers studying the same topic. I did this for success traits identified by the three researchers: Hill, McCoy, and St. John. The analysis is in Appendix D.

Hill found that there were 17 traits of successful people, while McCoy determined there were 12 and St. John eight (plus four secondary traits). Of St. John's eight, all matched one or both of Hill's and McCoy's. Three of St. John's findings were very similar to both Hill and McCoy's. All three agreed that having goals was a trait of success. Hill called it a "definite chief aim," McCoy found successful people are "decisive, disciplined goal setters," and St. John found "successful people have a specific focus." Moreover, all three alluded to having "enthusiasm" (Hill). McCoy found successful people "enjoy their work" and St. John discovered successful people "work hard while having fun." Finally, all three addressed "persistence" or as Hill termed it in 1928 "profiting by failure." McCoy found successful people "use negative experiences to discover their strengths. They're persistent," while St. John successful people "are persistent through failure." It should be noted that all three of these traits were discovered in the creation of the definition of success in Chapter 1.

When St. John's four secondary traits were considered, two additional traits had unanimous agreement. First, St. John said a "positive attitude" was important. McCoy found that successful people "have a positive attitude and plenty of confidence," and Hill in 1928 called it "self-confidence."

Second, St. John argued that "having mentors" was important, while McCoy found that successful people "surround themselves with competent, responsible and supportive people." On the other hand, Hill called this trait "the Mastermind," which he defined as *"when two people get together and work on a problem or towards a goal, a third mind* is created." I also put Hill's "cooperation" trait with his "Mastermind."

There were seven traits that were common to two of the authors—two for Hill and McCoy, three for Hill and St. John, and two for McCoy and St. John. In the meta-analysis Appendix D, I grouped Hill's "initiative and leadership" and "practicing the Golden Rule" into one trait and matched it with McCoy's successful people "have integrity and help others succeed." Likewise, I grouped Hill's "accurate thinking" and "concentration" into one and matched it with McCoy's successful people "develop good communication skills and problem-solving skills."

Hill's "imagination" could be matched with St. John's "successful people constantly come up with new ideas" and Hill's "habit of doing more than paid for" was matched with St. John's "successful people provide value to others." Moreover, Hill's "cosmic habit force" could be matched with St. John's successful people "are constantly getting better." This is synonymous with "continuous improvement," which I identified in Chapter 1 as being an important component of success. McCoy found successful people "have a sense of purpose and a desire to contribute to society," while St. John found successful people "are passionate about what they do." McCoy found that successful people "take risks" while one of St. John's secondary traits was "taking risks!"

Finally, there were six (four from Hill's 17 and two from McCoy's 12) that weren't found by either of the other authors. These included from Hill "the habit of saving," "self-control," "a pleasing personality," and "tolerance." Two traits that McCoy found while in my original pyramid and new formula were not mentioned by Hill or St. John. These were successful people "are heathy, have high energy levels, and schedule time to renew themselves" (physiology) and "believe in a higher power, or sometimes, just plain luck" (philosophy).

Trevor Blake, in his 2012 book *Three Simple Steps: A Map to Success in Business and Life*, writes that his three steps (could be traits) to success were: (1) reclaiming your mentality—"becoming the person you were born to be—an individual with the power to think for yourself and with an unlimited potential to achieve great things"; (2) creating winning ideas; and (3) transforming ideas into achievements.

John Wooden, the legendary UCLA basketball coach, is considered by many as the most successful coach ever. Over many years, he developed his Pyramid of Success model, which consisted of 15 "building blocks" and 10 "mortars." Wooden's model is basically a list of "success" traits.

The following is a content analysis of John Wooden's 15 "Building Blocks" + 10 "Mortars" (in italics) from his pyramid of success in the context of my own pyramid model:

Physiology

"**Condition** (physical health, endurance, strength, persistence)"
"**Skill** (ability, talent, expertise)"

Psychology

"**Industriousness** (sincerity, seriousness, hard work, application)"

"**Enthusiasm** (passion, eagerness, gusto, interest, excitement)"

"**Self-Control** (switch, regulator, controller)"

"**Alertness** (attentiveness, awareness, preparedness, vigilance)"

"**Initiative** (resourcefulness, creativity, inventiveness, idea)"

"**Intentness** (concentration, focus, attention)"

"**Poise** (composure, dignity, self-control, self-assurance, balance)"

"**Confidence** (sureness, poise, certainty, assurance)"

"***Ambition*** (drive, determination, motivation, desire)"

"***Adaptability*** (flexibility, malleability)"

"***Resourcefulness*** (imagination, creativity, originality)"

"***Fight*** (competition, contest)"

"***Patience*** (persistence, fortitude, endurance)"

"***Reliability*** (dependability, trustworthiness, steadfastness)"

Sociology

"**Friendship** (bond, relationship, attachment, companionship)"

"**Loyalty** (faithfulness, allegiance, trustworthiness, devotion)"

"**Cooperation** (collaboration, teamwork, assistance, help)"

Philosophy

"**Competitive Greatness** (merit, excellence, significance)"

"**Team Spirit** (atmosphere, essence, heart)"

"*Faith* (belief, conviction, commitment)"

"*Integrity* (honesty, truthfulness, reliability)"

"*Honesty* (goodness, trustworthiness, integrity, authenticity)"

"*Sincerity* (genuineness, honesty, authenticity)"

Wooden's 15 "building blocks" (traits) are skewed toward my psychology factor, with eight of the 15 being categorized as such and eight out of ten of the "mortars" being psychology. Of the 15 "building blocks," 12 were in my new definition of success and/or on Hill's, McCoy's, and St. John's lists. The three that were not were "team" related: Loyalty, Team Spirit, and Competitive Greatness. I suppose that these variables could (and maybe should) be included in a definition of success.

In addition to the 15 "building blocks" of the pyramid of success, there are 10 more traits that Wooden called "The Mortar," with five on each side. Only four of these 10 "mortars" (behaviors) were explicitly in my new definition of success and/ or on Hill's, McCoy's, and St. John's lists: Ambition (desire), Resourcefulness (imagination), Faith (belief), and Patience (persistence).

Now let's examine Sonja Lyubomirsky's list of "happiness activities" to check for any matches to traits that determine success in Wooden's model. Apparently, becoming "happy" is somewhat different from becoming "successful"! Only four (one-third) were a direct match: "Nurture Social Relationships," "Commit to Goals," "Practice Religion and Spirituality," and "Take Care of Your Body." Several others were implied: Lyubomirsky's "Express Gratitude," "Practice Acts of Kindness," "Learn to Forgive," and "Savor Life's Joys" could be part of the "Love" trait from my new definition and/or the research of Hill, McCoy, and St. John.

Moreover, Lyubomirsky's "Increase 'Flow' Experiences" could be the same as "Enthusiasm" which is an intense and eager enjoyment, interest, or approval of something. "Flow" probably ought to be on the list of success traits since it means being "in the zone," or the mental state in which a person performing some activity is fully immersed in a feeling of energized focus, full involvement, and enjoyment in the process of the activity. Finally, three activities or traits were not matches (but would be on the psychology side of my pyramid): (1) "Cultivate Optimism," a hopefulness and confidence about the future or the successful outcome of something; (2) "Avoid Overthinking"; and (3) "Develop Strategies for Coping."

Research indicates that perhaps nine out of 10 of the "successful" people who are interviewed about which trait(s) resulted in their success cannot with a high degree of confidence identify a single one! Since most successful people don't know or don't want to admit it might have been simply good luck, they guess. Many respond with worthy, but innocuous traits such as "hard work," "passion," "self-confidence," "focus" and "persistence." And while these traits do demonstrate some correlation with success, they usually do not contribute more to explaining or predicting success than luck.

Indeed, failures often exhibit the same positive traits. But people who fail are usually not interviewed, so the real reason(s) for success remain elusive or at the very least underreported. The findings of various success trait researchers over many decades seem to contradict each other though many employed the same or similar methodologies in determining traits. Nevertheless, trait theory can provide a significant amount of explanation and prediction for success.

So, what are the common traits of all successful people that are scientifically proven?

The following are traits *definitely* common to all successful people and fit in all four sides of my pyramid model:

- Successful people are decisive, disciplined goal setters, and have a specific focus.

- Successful people take risks.

- Successful people use negative experiences to discover their strengths.

- Successful people persist through failure and profit from it.

- Successful people enjoy their work and work hard while having fun.

- Successful people are enthusiastic, have a positive attitude and an abundance of self-confidence.

- Successful people surround themselves with competent, responsible, and supportive people and have mentors.

- Successful people have a sense of purpose, a desire to contribute to society, and are passionate about what they do.

It should be noted that successful people set goals. And all goals have risks. So, there could be failures. But if failures result in discovering new strengths or "profit," then the failures are worth enduring.

Research shows that the following traits are *most likely* common to all successful people and fit in all four sides of my pyramid model:

- They are healthy, have high energy levels, and schedule time to renew themselves.
- They have developed good communication and problem-solving skills.
- They have initiative, imagination, and consistently come up with new ideas.
- They have integrity, help others succeed, and practice the Golden Rule.
- They provide value to others and have the habit of doing more than paid for.
- They believe in a higher power, or sometimes, just plain luck.
- They are constantly getting better.

While the above 15 traits are scientifically proven, there are others that have empirical support. In addition to traits in the new definition of success and in my original 1976 model, others should include (1) self-control (moderation), (2) determination, (3) extroversion, and (4) conscientiousness.

Researchers led by Timothy Judge, PhD, now a professor in the Fisher College of Business at The Ohio State University, conducted a meta-analysis of success studies and found that extroversion is the best predictor of success followed closely by conscientiousness.

Extroversion is a measure of how much energy a person derives from socialization with others. Extroverts tend to get along well with others, enjoy meeting new people, making friends, and are generally energized by being around people (and are exposed to many opportunities). They often have high self-esteem and are action-oriented, energetic, optimistic, talkative, assertive, outgoing, good-natured, enthusiastic, and very comfortable in social situations. At the same time, extroverts need to be careful that they do not become bored, restless, or seem attention-seeking, easily distracted, or unable to spend time alone (this is a critical variable for success). It should be remembered that extroversion is on a continuum. It's not a case of "you either have it or you don't."

The "conscientiousness" trait shows how thoughtful, goal-oriented, and controlled an individual is (the Psychology side of my pyramid). Moreover, conscientiousness implies a desire to do a task well, aim for achievement, to take obligations to others seriously (Sociology side) and deliver on promises. On the Physiology side, a conscientious person is often very immaculate in appearance/grooming. If you are high on conscientiousness, you are systematic, hardworking, reliable, careful, efficient, disciplined, deliberate, responsible, diligent, organized, thorough, dependable, persistent, and tend to aim for achievement through planning and self-discipline.

A person with a high level of conscientiousness makes plans and preserves when faced with hardships. If you are low in conscientiousness, however, you tend to procrastinate and be easy-going, laid back, less goal-oriented, disorderly, more impulsive, spontaneous, and sometimes reckless. Though extreme conscientiousness can result in you becoming a workaholic, a perfectionist, or compulsive, scientific studies have found that high levels of conscientiousness results in better health, well-being, and higher productivity.

According to Rory Vaden, "Successful people have the self-discipline to do things they don't want to do. They do the things they don't want to do *even when* they don't *feel like* doing them." Further, Vaden writes "Of all qualities, self-discipline is one special quality that will guarantee you greater successes, bigger accomplishments, and more fulfilling happiness. Of a thousand principles for success developed over the ages, this one quality or practice will do more to assure that you accomplish wonderful things with your life than any other."

Let's now take a look at how these traits come together in various success formulas, where they are given different weights and ratios depending on the variables involved. Reviewing a comprehensive inventory of such formulas will make it easier to arrive at a scientific formula for authentic success.

CHAPTER 5

"IT'S ALWAYS DARKEST BEFORE THE DAWN"

New Formula, an Amazing Discovery, and Why It Works!

I have experienced a lot of "progress and setbacks" developing a "workable" general theory (model/formula) for "authentic" success that would be effective for most people who tried it. My first model (the Personal Marketing Pyramid) that I developed in 1976 included fewer than one-fourth of the variables that scientific research now shows results in success. The first ten or so models I developed over a four-year period held much more promise. However, I quickly discovered "serious flaws" with all those formulas regarding their ability to correctly predict or explain who would or would not become successful.

At one point, I was almost convinced that success was (1) just random (a result of luck, chance or a "happy accident"); (2) all genetic; (3) granted by a Supreme Being (God, divine intervention, universal intelligence, or karma); (4) a combination of luck, happenstance, DNA and God; (5) different for different kinds of success (entrepreneurial success would

152 | THE SUCCESS PYRAMID

require different variables than spiritual success); or (6) just impossible to completely understand or, to paraphrase the saying by Winston Churchill about Russia, a "*riddle*, wrapped in a *mystery*, inside an *enigma*!" It was then that I recalled that many innovative breakthroughs occurred when people were about to give up ("darkest before the dawn").

That's when I decided to look at existing formulas for success. The following are some formulas for success I found online.

S = Goals + Habits

Source: Career Vision

Goals provide direction and help you focus. Habits help you achieve goals. If you don't have explicit (SMART) goals and good habits, you won't become successful. The likelihood of success increases with SMART goals and the formation of good habits.

S = Passion + Purpose + People

Source: Success.com

A "True Success Formula" consists of three pillars that are essential for authentic success:

1. Passion: positive energy even during tough times

2. Purpose: having meaning in your life

3. People: optimizing your relationships

$S = G \times 10$

Source: Grant Cardone

The 10X formula for success is: *Set goals that are 10 times bigger than the average, then work 10 times harder than average to achieve them.* Cardone refers to the latter as taking "massive" action. It takes extraordinary thinking and effort to achieve extraordinary success.

Talent x Effort = Skill | Skill x Effort = Achievement (S)

Source: Angela Duckworth

"Skill, or how good you are at something, isn't just something you're born with. Skill is the product of talent or potential in something multiplied by how much effort you put into it. Achievement or success is taking that skill and putting even more effort into it."

$S = \text{Work} + \text{Play} + \text{Keep Mouth Shut}$

Source: Albert Einstein

What is Einstein's formula for success in life? "If A is success in life, then $A = x + y + z$. Work is x, Play is y, and z is Keeping your mouth shut."

S = E.N.G.A.G.E.

Source: Francesco Marconi

E = Explore your meaning; N = Narrow your goals; G = Generate a plan; A = Anticipate roadblocks; G = Gain persistence; E = Elevate yourself.

S = Ability x Effort x Attitude

Source: Kazuo Inamori

This simple success equation suggests that the outcome of your life, work, studies, hobbies, etc., is the product of three factors: ability, effort, and attitude. The maximum score you can achieve is 100 x 100 x 100 = 1,000,000.

S = Right Attitude + Realistic Goals + Winning Charisma + Willpower + Mental Strength

Source: Experteer

These are five traits that the most successful people share; cultivating them will help you achieve your goals.

S = IQ x EQ

Source: Top 20 Training

"EQ = Thinking + Learning + Communicating. An important part of life is problem-solving, and most of life's problems are EQ related. We know that when adults fail in the real world, it is usually not because they lack intelligence, but because they are unable to work effectively with other people. This is even more true in our family lives and friendships."

S = (Thoughts + Ideas + Goals + Action) x Perseverance

Source: Spencer Sekulin

"The major ingredients of success are universal and eternal—and they are available to everyone." See this excellent *Medium*

article: https://medium.com/the-ascent/heres-the-formula
-for-success-d37c1b84bed2.

E + R = O (Events + Responses = Outcome)

Source: Jack Canfield

"Successful people take a different approach to events. They simply change their responses (R) to the events (E) until they get the outcomes (O) they want. You can change your thinking, change your communication, change the pictures you hold in your head (your images of the world) and you can change your behavior (the things you do). That's all you really have control over anyway."

S = Dreams x Goals x Learning x Plan x Action

Source: ActionCOACH Brad Sugars

"People who achieve great things typically use a systemized approach."

S = C + M + C

Source: Samar Sisodia (Quora)

"*Clarity* – Successful people have clarity of why they are doing what they are doing and then stick to it."

"*Mindset* – I have not seen any successful person with a weak mindset. They work on their mindset every day and build stronger habits. They are known to work on themselves much harder than they do on others."

"*Consistency* – Well, if you take any field, every successful person tends to show up every day in their line of work and be consistent."

$$S = D + G + S + P + T$$

Source: Joel Stein (Quora)

D = "Dreams—big dreams."

G = "Goals—know where you are going."

S = "Study and focus on the area where your goals are."

P = "Perseverance—everybody has a dream. Everybody has a goal. Many study their area of interest and focus, but very few persevere until attaining it."

T = "Thankful—be always thankful; the more you give, the more you receive."

Strategy + Execution (with Consistency) = Results

Source: Joelle K. Jay (Inc.com)

Strategy – "Ask yourself: On a scale from one to 10, do you believe you have the right strategy for your business?"

Execution – "Ask yourself: On a scale from one to 10, are you executing the strategy well enough for it to pay off?"

S = 1 <thing> per week for 5–10 years

Source: Tim Denning

"A singular focus you have for 5–10 years will allow you to achieve mastery. You're bound to develop the skills, network, and strategies to succeed because time is working for you. Is this the same as deliberate practice?"

$$S = G + A + (see\ red)?$$

Source: Ann Marie Smith

"Everyone is searching for a formula for success, but there is no one single formula for everyone, as our needs, wants, and wishes vary from individual to individual. On the other hand, it is noteworthy to mention that those who have achieved success have many qualities in common. The attributes of *vision, risk-taking, passion, planning, focus, and perseverance* are typically utilized in various proportions to accomplish success. On the journey to success, the first timer must identify a goal, as the goal determines your actions."

$$IR^{\circ}_{p} <=== PBC = Goals + (S\ \&\ K)A,$$
$$where\ A = (v + b)\ and\ 88\%(f)c$$

Source: RPC Leadership Associates

IR°_{p} – "Improved results—organizational and/or personal—is our ultimate outcome."

PBC – "Positive Behavior Change drives Improved Results. It is important to focus on the positive aspects of behavior change since over 75% of our attitudes are based on negative influences in our lives."

Goals – "crucial to successfully achieving improved results. Because goals address only the What and Why; they alone will not get us there."

S & K – "We all need Skills and Knowledge in both our professional and personal lives. They address the How (skills) and the Where and When (knowledge). Even with goals, we are not where we want to be for improved results."

A – "Our Attitudes are Habits of Thought and are a function of our Values (v) and our Beliefs (b). Nearly 95% of our Attitudes were developed by the time we were 5 years old and are predominately negative in nature. Attitudes are our Want to Improve Results and combined with Skills, Knowledge and Goals enable us to drive Positive Behavior Change."

88%(f)c – "As much as 88% of our decisions are made below the conscious level—a function of prior conditioning. We don't even think about how we do most things (tying our shoes, driving a car, etc.), including those that hinder us from achieving our goals."

S (Flywheel Effect) = Focus x Faith x Effort

E.g., 50% X 50% X 50% = 12.5% needs to be 98% X 98% X 98% = 94%!

Source: Flywheel Effect—Jim Collins | Formula: Cameron Herold

"The Flywheel effect is a concept developed in the book *Good to Great*. No matter how dramatic the end result, good-to-great transformations never happen in one fell swoop. In building a great company or social sector enterprise, there is no single defining action, no grand program, no one killer innovation, no solitary lucky break, no miracle moment. Rather, the process resembles relentlessly pushing a giant, heavy flywheel, turn upon turn, building momentum until a point of break-through, and beyond."

$$S = W + A + E + C$$

Source: Tony Robbins

W is specifically what you want, A is massive action, E is evaluating the action, and C is continuing or changing approach.

"The truth of the matter is that there's nothing you can't accomplish if: 1) You clearly decide what it is that you're absolutely committed to achieving, 2) You are willing to take massive action, 3) You notice what's working or not, and 4) You continue to change your approach until you achieve what you want, using whatever life gives you along the way."

$$S = \text{Hard Work} + \text{Skill} + \text{Advantage} + \text{Luck}$$

Source: CFA Institute

"Hard work could be 50% (35% of respondents) or 75% (33% of respondents); 16% said less than 50% and 16% more than 75%. Advantage is also considered privilege (i.e., coming from a wealthy family)."

$$S = \text{Self-belief} + \text{Plan of Action That Is Researched} + \text{Massive Effort}$$

Source: Jim Rohn

"You have attracted the things to you because of the person you have become. If you will change (inside), everything else will change."

S = Repetition + Connecting Experiences + Learning to Say "No" + Doing What You Love

Source: Steve Jobs

"To master something, you need to be patient and work hard. You'll get better at something the more times you practice it. If you ask creative people how they did something so unique, they will feel a little guilty because they didn't really do it entirely. They saw something that led to innovation. That's because they had mastered the art of connecting experiences and synthesizing new things. Don't hesitate to say, 'No, I don't want to,' or 'I won't.' Be straightforward. Sometimes this is the best approach. Jobs concluded that successful people were passionate about their work and persevered, especially when circumstances were highly challenging."

S = Hard Work + Focus + Concentration + Interest

S = Smart Work + Different Thoughts + Creativity

S = Meditation + Workout + Reading – Overthinking – Negativity

Source: Unknown

These final three formulas suggest that smart or other (deliberate) work is important.

While I had already discovered most of the components contained in these formulas, there were a few I had overlooked: (1) consistency (just show up!), (2) charisma, (3) growth mindset, (4) repetition, (5) doing what you love, and (6) connecting experiences to synthesize new things. Though I knew there were at least 30 scientifically confirmed traits that impacted personal success, I still didn't know how they fit together or interacted.

It was also interesting to note that Angela Duckworth had scientifically proven (in her 2016 book *Grit: The Power of Passion and Perseverance*) that in addition to having resiliency and being hardworking, the combination of passion and perseverance (or what she called "grit") was a defining factor in all kinds of success. Yet only three of the 24 online formulas for success mentioned specifically the word "passion," although several mentioned to "do what you love." Only twice were the words "perseverance" or "persistence" mentioned. These two variables separately and in combination have an abundance of empirical evidence that they contribute to people becoming successful.

I had almost given up again when I looked at the book *Three Feet from Gold*. This book took its title from the story told by Napoleon Hill in his book *Think and Grow Rich* about a man who gave up and sold his gold mine when it appeared that the rich vein he had been mining had run out. However, the man who bought his mine (for pennies on the dollar) hired an engineer (expert) who found that the major vein picked up again just three feet away where it had appeared to stop.

So, I "hired" more experts in the form of additional books and videos. It is truly ridiculous how much money I have invested in research materials for this book (some of which were of little value even though the testimonials, "sample" chapter(s), and/or table of contents looked promising). As a professor, I was able to "borrow" many of the extremely expensive, out-of-print, or esoteric books through interlibrary loan.

I was extremely grateful for this service, as it saved me a lot of money (even when I paid the return postage). However, I ended up purchasing more than half of these books, as the loan period was often too short for me to add items to the different parts of my book.

Even though the additional reference materials helped, I was very discouraged that I was still unable to develop a "formula" or a general theory for success. Then, I remembered that progress is often possible if one ventures beyond one's own areas of expertise. So, I did that! I carefully examined research findings from the social sciences (especially psychology and sociology), happiness, business (especially personal branding), leadership, entrepreneurship, network science, and other disciplines (especially physiology, philosophy, religion and even "self-care" in nursing and occupational therapy research). And "patterns" began to slowly emerge.

A third thing I did was I finally admitted to myself that a formula for success wasn't going to be just adding a few variables like many of the formulas cataloged above, or my original pyramid formula that was based on the life balance theory (Chapter 3) combined with Trait Theory (Chapter 4), balance and synergy. Recall my 1976 model was Success = (Physiology + Psychology + Sociology + Philosophy) x Balance. Each of the four sciences contained traits (or resources) common to all four, as well as several unique to each science. Moreover, it became clear that an effective formula for success wasn't going to be simple, like the formula for happiness: $H = .50S + .10C + .40V$, where (H) stands for happiness and is equal to the *sum* of one's genetic set-range for happiness (S), a person's life circumstances (C), and factors under their voluntary (V)

"IT'S ALWAYS DARKEST BEFORE THE DAWN" | 163

control.[10] But my new success formula would incorporate my original model and include elements from happiness research.

After over another year of full-time research, my formula for success already had 12 variables and I was pretty sure there were more. The reason for so many was that the research showed that each had some empirical (scientific) support. Recall that separately the life balance theory accounts for between 5 and 10 percent of people who try it faithfully actually succeeding, and trait theory accounts for roughly the same percent. Combined, these theories can predict and/or explain only up to one-fifth of why some people become successful and others don't—even with similar life balance and traits.

I found early on that success was not correlated with any demographic variable (including age, gender, education, race, ethnicity, religion, social class). However, (1) having a high IQ, (2) being handsome or good looking, and/or (3) having wealth, unused time, and other resources could provide an easier path to becoming successful. Indeed, Paula J. Caproni, in her book *The Science of Success,* found that IQ beyond a certain level was of no value as a predictor of future success. And perhaps being handsome was an "advantage" because other people "help" good-looking people because it feels good to be around beauty. Nevertheless, the research showed the "handsome" person must eventually "produce" to remain successful (since beauty fades over time).

While I found no causality between success and income or existing wealth, I did find it was easier for wealthy people to become successful since they could purchase needed resources

---

10. Seligman, 2002; 2010.

(i.e., concentrated resources theory) that increase their odds of success. For example, a wealthy person can enhance his "success" by paying to have his autobiography or a popular book "ghostwritten." In addition to money, I found that the more time (another resource) a person has available to enhance the salient variables in the four sides of the pyramid, the greater the odds for success. Nevertheless, scientific evidence suggests that pretty much anybody can become successful regardless of their demographic profile.

Interestingly, my research revealed that most people don't know the qualities that caused them to be successful in the first place (and this is the main reason trait theory is so fraught with error). In fact, many people can say only that there was a *correlation* between certain skills, behaviors, traits, or other factors that led to their success. But as every scientist knows or quickly learns—correlation is *not* causation.

This is why I believe most success studies are seriously flawed—successful people (or those who repeatedly fail) don't really know how or why they became successful (or fail), and therefore almost all guess at the reason(s). Some people are absolutely convinced that they know the reason(s) for their success or failure, however. In virtually every case, the top reasons for success and failure are the same: "hard work" or didn't work hard enough, "passion" or wasn't passionate enough, and "persistence" or didn't stick with it! Who can argue that these traits/factors are *not* crucial for success or wouldn't "cause" failure?

And now thanks to Duckworth and other researchers, there is empirical evidence. Moreover, many people, when pressed further, will credit "luck" as one of the significant causes, if not the main cause, of their success (or bad luck for failure).

This usually ends the discussion because for many people, the causes of their success(es) or failure(s) are truly a mystery. And because scientists don't have a lot of statistical confidence in their findings, there is a lot of speculation, conjecture, and inferences made from the little available (and often contradictory) empirical data.

AN AMAZING DISCOVERY

When I took another look at the traits from the definition of success developed in Chapter 1 and started to categorize them into the four sides of my pyramid model, I witnessed an astonishing feature. I had hypothesized that several traits would apply to more than one side and some to all sides. Several years after developing the new definition in Chapter 1 and while editing the chapter on traits, I had an "eureka" moment! The epiphany was: *All* the traits in my new definition of success are found in all four sides of my pyramid model!

The following are traits from the definition of success in Chapter 1 common to all four sides of my pyramid model:

1. Demonstrate love (gratitude, giving, and receiving) and passion

2. Utilize "quiet time," hard but enjoyable work, "grit," and the help of others

3. Recognize and seize quality ideas/opportunities

4. Plan, prepare, and exchange resources (time, money, deliberate practice) to differentiate

5. Position, balance, and visualize written SMART goals/intentions/promises

6. Assume risks and enthusiastically act to enhance continuous improvement

7. Overcome, profit from failures, be determined and persist (persevere)

8. Develop positive and disciplined habits, including self-control

9. Influence your and your target audience's fun, life-satisfaction, well-being, and happiness

10. Simplify and reduce stress

The following is a discussion of each of the traits common to all four sides and how you can specifically utilize each to enhance your authentic success attainment.

1. Demonstrate Love, Giving, Gratitude, and Passion.

Richard Braunstein said, "It is possible to give without loving, but it is impossible to love without giving." I never really considered love a viable trait for success until I had a eureka moment while teaching an honors course on the science of success in Fall 2022. Earlier versions of my model had love as a possible trait in the Sociology (Emotional) side of my pyramid, especially as it related to family members.

Although love was in a few definitions of success I found online, my research beginning in Fall 2022 clearly demonstrated that love was the most important resource that a person who desired to succeed authentically could possess! This included an enthusiastic love for all virtues in the four sides of the pyramid, including your body (even though it may not be like you would want—but you get only one and are stuck with it), your work (even though there may be some frustrations), your mental competencies, friends, family, significant others in your networks and God, a supreme being, Infinite Intelligence or other philosophical virtue(s) that you find important. Having love also entails having a passion, purpose, mission, vision or "calling" for your life. Love, like many resources, can be acquired through spending time in nature, meditating, and deliberately cultivating it. Refer to Chapter 6 for a deeper dive into this trait.

In addition to demonstrating love, the successful person is grateful for what he or she has achieved and doesn't compare his or her success to others. Science confirms that life is really a game of giving and receiving—whatever you send out in word or action will return to you (good or bad), and the more you give, the more you receive! Yes, it is a paradox, but true! The Dead Sea is a dead sea because it continually receives and never gives!

2. Utilize "Quiet Time," Hard but Enjoyable Work, "Grit," and the Help of Others.

Several researchers, including Trevor Blake, discuss the importance of "taking quiet time." As Blake says on his website, "All you need is a quiet space, a few minutes of your time, and a willingness to focus on your breath." Blake intentionally avoids calling this practice "meditation" because of the latter term's association with "woo woo" behaviors, but it is essentially the same idea. As he writes, "Meditation is simply the act of being present, in the moment, letting go of distracting thoughts, and giving life the space it needs to commune with you. It's about learning to observe your thoughts and emotions without getting caught up in them. And the best part is that anyone can do it."

In virtually every survey ever conducted with successful people, respondents have listed "hard work" as one of the traits most associated with their success. And the most successful people really enjoy their work! Most successful people consider their work a "calling" and have a passion for their jobs. Further, research shows that while talent, luck, and opportunities contribute to success, it is the relentless pursuit of one's goals through focused hard work (deliberate practice) that is the "golden key."

Duckworth was correct when she found that "no matter the domain, the highly successful had a kind of ferocious determination that played out in two ways. First, these exemplars were unusually resilient and hardworking. Second, they knew in a very, very deep way what it was they wanted. They not only had determination, they had *direction*. It was this combination of passion and perseverance that made high achievers special. In a word, they had grit."

Moreover, research shows that behind every successful person is someone who helped them (and often it is quoted that behind every successful man is a strong woman—a wife, mother, sister, mentor, or friend).

Finally, research also shows that if you spend enough time helping other people become successful, you will achieve success in the process. About 100 years ago, Napoleon Hill wrote, "It is literally true that you can succeed best and quickest by helping others to succeed." Further, Jon Gordon said, "You are not a true success unless you are helping others be successful." Similarly, there is a Hindu proverb that says, "Help thy brother's boat across, and lo! thine own has reached the shore." This is a paradox but true.

3. Recognize and Seize Quality Ideas, Opportunities, and Experiences.

A successful person is always on the lookout for great ideas and opportunities to advance his or her professional and personal success. There are seven questions to ask when you are considering an idea/opportunity: (1) is it unique, (2) is it needed, (3) is it demanded, (4) can it be value priced, (5) is it scalable, (6) can you do it better than the competition, and (7) are you passionate about the idea or opportunity? Researchers agree the best ideas/opportunities are imaginative, innovative, and creative and that you determine your opportunities (or lack thereof if you unknowingly have a weak or negative personal brand). Steve Jobs argued that you need to connect experiences (ideas or opportunities) to synthesize new things. Refer to Chapter 6 for a deeper dive into this trait.

4. Plan, Prepare, and Exchange Resources to Differentiate Yourself.

In addition to love and gratitude, each person possesses a set of unique skills, talents, or resources in each of the four sides of the pyramid. This combination not only contributes to or detracts from your personal efficacy, but it also differentiates you from others—which can either build your network or discourage others from supporting your cause. It is critical that you know your "current" image, both online and off. A good first step is to type your name into a search engine, like Google (I did this and found 51 unique items online about myself—fortunately all were positive). The old saying is true: "You never get a second chance to make a good first impression."

Next, evaluate your existing resources or "strengths and weaknesses" (the SW of a personal SWOT analysis, or what an accountant might view as assets and liabilities). Doing this will greatly assist you in creating or enhancing authentic success and turning "failures" into successes. You might find that you can purchase, borrow, or trade for a resource that you need to make yourself better.

As an example, assess how you use your time. We all get 24 hours a day—which is the only resource I can think of that is equally distributed—for work, sleep, exercise, meditation or quiet time, stress reduction, knowledge acquisition, professional development, socializing, giving, and leaving a legacy.

You can extend your time on the earth beyond the average of 26,000 days (at the time of this writing, I have already lived about 24,450 days—so I need to get busy on achieving my purpose!). Ways to manage time wisely include "purchasing" time-saving products, services, or methods; hiring out mundane responsibilities; or just "choosing your battles."

Research shows that using money (though not a strong determinant of authentic success), being determined, not wasting resources, and having self-control can enhance the development of success. Doing an inventory will clearly show the areas of your life that are going well, those that need attention, those that need to be exchanged, or those that may be outsourced. The Pareto Distribution (or the 80/20 Rule) often applies: 80 percent of your outcomes are due to the 20 percent of your efforts that truly matter. Focusing on the most productive tasks will result in greater output since so much of your output is determined by a relatively small amount of what you do each day (the 20 percent). Often a modest improvement in a seemingly insignificant area of the pyramid could have a dramatic impact on your overall success. For instance, improving your posture, updating your signature line for your emails, or laughing more often could create a positive synergistic effect on all four sides of the pyramid.

An easy way to differentiate yourself is to write a Unique Value Proposition (UVP). You have a purpose that only you can fulfill. Once your distinguishing features have been identified and inventoried (or if you are still not sure, ask trusted friends to share descriptors of you), you should write a mission statement or, better yet, a one-sentence mantra based on this UVP. While your brand is not a tagline or a slogan, a well-defined UVP can enhance your recognition as an expert; increase your reputation, credibility, and self-confidence; and advance your career or personal success. I developed a mantra based on my four greatest strengths (traits) and use it to guide me both in my professional and personal life:

> *Work hard. Live simply.*
> *Give generously. Laugh often.*

5. Position, Balance, and Visualize Written SMART Goals/ Intentions/Promises.

After you have determined what you want to be known for and made sure that your UVP is cohesive, clear, and consistent, the next step is to devote resources to challenging and SMART (Specific, Measurable, Attainable, Relevant and Time-based) goals. Grant Cardone advocated the "10x formula for success," which is to set goals that are 10 times bigger than the average, then work 10 times harder than average to achieve them.

Research shows that successful people have a clear vision of what they want to achieve. Napoleon Hill called this a "definite chief aim" and said that it had to be much more than a "wish." There had to be a "burning desire" for achieving the definite goal.

The main takeaway from this suggestion for success is that you must visualize actually achieving your goals. In other words, you need to form a picture or mental image of the successful result of your goal. For example, you should "visualize" what it is going to "feel" like when you win. You should never visualize losing or even making mistakes or having a poor performance, as this increases the likelihood that you will actually do those negative things. You should train yourself to picture what you want to happen, instead of what you don't. When you visualize winning, your chances of success increase dramatically. Finally, research shows that visualizing positive outcomes can increase a person's confidence.

Overall, you must be determined, dedicated, have willpower, grit, and resolve to achieve your goals, intentions, or promises. A person seeking to develop authentic success should endeavor to create a balance and enhance synergy in the four sides of the pyramid—physiology, psychology, sociology, and philosophy. For instance, there is scientific evidence that genetics plays a major role in how physically attractive a person is and that good-looking people have an advantage in becoming successful. Nevertheless, you will be much more successful than the attractive person who might score a perfect 10 in physiology but would be below average in the other three areas. The Goldilocks Principle certainly applies: you want all four sides of your pyramid to be "just right"!

174 | THE SUCCESS PYRAMID

6. Assume Risks and Enthusiastically Act to Enhance Continuous Improvement.

All actions have risks, and sometimes the most gigantic efforts fail. But researchers have found that people with the most failures who persevere and persist frequently end up being the most successful. In his 2006 book *Billionaire: Secrets to Success*, Bill Bartmann admitted to having several ups and downs. He was a millionaire three times, bankrupt twice, and a billionaire once. Bartmann died in 2016 as a result of complications from surgery.

While major actions may be necessary at times, the most beneficial seem to be micro actions or achieving many small wins. All actions should center on developing a consistent look, message, and presence online and off and on all four sides of the pyramid. This can be best accomplished by deliberate practice. For example, you might increase your circle of influence by creating a website on which you share your story or start a blog to highlight some of your expertise and grow your network and online presence.

Regarding continuous improvement (in all four sides of the pyramid), James Clear said, "If you get one percent better each day for one year, you'll end up thirty-seven times better by the time you're done." Successful people are constantly seeking to learn and improve their skills and knowledge. They are open to new ideas and experiences and are willing to adapt to changing circumstances. Research shows continuous improvement in achieving success is enhanced by writing down (preferably in a journal) your progress, big and small wins, setbacks, or outright failures. For instance, I share my story on a blog and keep a gratitude journal.

Finally, the role of luck and genetics cannot be underestimated when taking action toward a goal. For example, research by Michael J. Mauboussin, in his 2012 book *The Success Equation,* has shown that the contribution of luck is 38 percent in the National Football League, but 53 percent in the National Hockey League. So, skill accounts for only 62 percent of winning a football game but less than 50 percent for winning a hockey game. This is why the underdog often wins!

7. Overcome, Profit from Failures, Be Determined and Persist.

There exists scientific proof that previous failures may be just as important as a string of successes. Hill argues, "Every adversity, every failure, every heartache carries with it the seed of an equal or greater benefit." Moreover, Hill writes, "Opportunity often comes disguised in the form of misfortune, or temporary defeat." Successful people are willing to put in the effort to overcome and profit from failure and keep pushing through obstacles. It takes unflinching determination to succeed. Determination is positive emotional motivation of persevering toward achieving challenging goals despite the obstacles.

In his 2023 book *Power of Persistence,* John Martin writes, "It has been proven throughout history that persistence—not talent—is the most valuable ingredient to accomplishing feats both big and small." Martin presents a simple seven-step formula for breaking the cycle of starting and quitting. Martin reminds us that quitting is the only "true" failure in life. There is also wisdom in the quote by Vince Lombardi: "Never give up in any situation. The winners never quit and quitters never win." When you want something badly enough, you must persevere. Like most resources, perseverance and persistence can be learned.

8. Develop Positive and Disciplined Habits including Self-Control.

Positive and disciplined habits result from achieving goals. The 21/90 rule states that it takes 21 days to make a habit and 90 days to make it a permanent lifestyle change. However, scientific research has revealed that the 21-day rule to form a new habit is a myth. In a study published in the *European Journal of Social Psychology,* researchers found that it takes an average of 66 days for a new behavior to become a habit.

Finally, the best habit to attain is self-control—the ability to control one's emotions and desires or the expression of them in one's behavior, especially in difficult situations. The three types of self-control are (1) impulse control, (2) emotional control, and (3) movement control—staying still when needed and out of other people's personal space. Mastering all three types is essential for success attainment because emotions influence the decisions we make.

There is a saying (by anonymous) that contains much wisdom about impulse and emotional control: "Never make a permanent decision based on a temporary emotion." Oscar Wilde is credited with saying, "I don't want to be at the mercy of my emotions. I want to use them, to enjoy them, and to dominate them." Every successful person should do likewise.

Frank Outlaw said, "Watch your thoughts, they become words; watch your words, they become actions; watch your actions, they become habits; watch your habits, they become character; watch your character, for it becomes your destiny."

Regarding movement control, I have a dear friend who gets into everyone's personal space. I and others will back up, but she will continue her movement forward until we hit a wall! She claims she must get so close because she doesn't hear well. But it is irritating to have someone in your face, especially during flu season.

9. Influence Your and Your Target Audience's Fun, Life-Satisfaction, Well-Being, and Happiness.

Once you have clarity about what makes you unique, you are ready to distinguish yourself from the competition and position yourself as an authority in your chosen work to a well-defined target audience. Understanding your competitors' unique value propositions can assist you in communicating and offering value that the competitors don't or don't do adequately. Use multiple touchpoints (can be defined as any form of communication that others can interact with you) to make it easy for your target audience to choose you over the competition, to offer recommendations or endorsements, or to engage with you directly or via your online platforms (such as your website or an app). A careful and honest evaluation and reflection can often reveal how well you are positively influencing your target audience's and your own life-satisfaction, well-being, and happiness.

Finally, an often-overlooked trait that fits into all four sides of the pyramid is having a sense of humor, having fun, and laughing. It has been said that humans are the only creatures on earth endowed with the power of laughter. Other research revealed that children laugh on average 300 to 400 times a day, while adults laugh fewer than 30 or 40 times a day! Play is also important. Since researchers argue that success is a journey, you should play and have fun along the way!

10. Simplify and Reduce Stress.

In his 2014 book *Dial it Down, Live it Up: 8 Steps to Simplify Your Life*, Jeff Davidson discusses several practical techniques for simplifying one's life. Specifically, (1) solutions often lie within the problem; (2) you have to want only what you really need; (3) reduce the number of choices and create checklists to help you avoid choice overload; (4) devote attention to issues or problems that are important; (5) do enough research, but don't do extensive research when working on an issue; (6) tap into gut instincts and listen; (7) determine what you can get rid of, since you will feel the freest when possessions are few; and (8) when you add one item, remove one item (on a personal note this is hard for me to do).

Davidson reminds us that "Even if things haven't gone so well, from this moment on is a new beginning. Decide what you want to do next, and don't be surprised if you feel invigorated."

I've been intrigued by books such as Debbie Ford's *The Best Year of Your Life: Dream It, Plan It, Live It* (2005), Stephen Levine's *A Year to Live: How to Live This Year As If It Were Your Last* (1997), and Kerry & Chris Shook's *One Month to Live:*

Thirty Days to a No-Regrets Life (2008). The premise of each book is that people are often completely unprepared for their death and feel badly for not having had great relationships, finding and doing their "calling" or passion, becoming more spiritual, or experiencing real joy. More than 9,000 people die every day in the US. It does make sense to live each day as if it is your last.

My next steps were to (1) "map" the success process and (2) re-examine the variables I had in my original pyramid model.

> SUCCESS = (1) Burning Desire for something (i.e., authentic success would be your passion, purpose, calling, what gives you "flow," your true north; write it down and look at and think about achieving it every day, even many times during the day) → (2) Show love for the desire and everything and everyone connected with it (I know this sounds "mushy" but it is critical for success) → (3) List what it will take to achieve this "desire" (i.e., goal, intention, promise, dream), be willing to do whatever it takes, and inventory your current resources and how you can leverage them to achieve this desire (i.e., money, time, skills, deliberate practice). If you don't have the resources, how will you acquire them? Borrow? Exchange?) → (4) Believe that you can achieve this desire, (5) Break the "desire" (i.e., goal, intention, promise) into "achievable" parts, be SMART about what must be done and in what order → (6) Work hard and take actions

daily (i.e., either micro, medium, or major) to achieve small wins or continuous progress (don't go to bed at night until have achieved something toward attaining this goal) → (7) Get initial support, (8) Display grit and be persistent and turn failures into wins and wins into habits.

Below you'll see the original variables included in my pyramid model. I stressed in 1976 a holistic approach to success achievement and am certain that developing the whole person (with balance and synergy) is relevant today (50 plus years later). This included a healthy body, mind, EQ, and soul. Over the next few years, I added some characteristics (items in *italics*). These included traits such as a growth mindset, initial support, frugality/simplicity, and enjoyment of life. However, I was still unable to develop a model that if followed would result in a majority of people becoming successful.

The following shows constructs of success hypothesized by me (1976–2023) in my pyramid model:

Physiology (Body)

- Nutrition/Water
- Rest/Sleep
- Exercise
- Clothing
- Grooming/Cleanliness
- Posture

- Attractiveness
- Laughter/Play/Fun
- *Stress management*

Psychology (Mind)

- Reading
- Education/Knowledge
- Games
- Laughter/Play/Fun
- *Self-confidence*
- *Growth mindset*

Sociology (Emotions)

- Relationships/Others first
- Family
- Friends/*Companionship*
- Coworkers/mentors
- Followers
- Organizations
- *Initial support*
- *Networking*
- *Reciprocity*

Philosophy (Soul)

- Religion/Faith/Belief
- Praying/Meditation
- Ethics/Morals/Integrity
- Giving/*Charity*/*Gratitude*
- *Enjoyment of life*
- *Leaving a legacy*
- *Kindness*
- *Frugality/Simplicity*
- *Wisdom*

When I thought all hope was lost, everything seemed to come together on December 2, 2022 (the date I received a horrible cancer diagnosis) and the final "formula" became clear. *So, after 50 years of part-time work and several years of full-time research, I believe I have created a formula that has a higher probability than any other previously created equation for obtaining true, authentic, sustainable, or long-term success!*

Though I have no access to an appropriate dataset, or the years needed to collect primary data for a full-scale regression analysis, the previous research and my findings suggest the following formula (regression line) in this order.

$$S = L + O + V + E$$

My research suggests these approximate percentages for each of the four variables: about 40 percent love/gratitude/giving/

passion, about 25 percent opportunity/idea, about 20 percent visualization (of goals), and about 15 percent execution/action/persistence. I am not a big fan of mnemonic devices (i.e., success equaling the word "love"), but it does make the formula difficult to forget!

More specifically, success is equal to the sum of (L) Love/Gratitude/Giving/Passion (of self – physiology; of knowledge – psychology; of other people and creatures/nature – sociology and of wisdom – philosophy) times balance divided by four; (O) Opportunity/Idea minus luck; (V) Visualization of already achieving goals times persistence divided by four; and (E) Execution of actions in the four areas – physiology, psychology, sociology and philosophy times a "willingness to do whatever it takes," exchange or grit divided by four.

While it may appear complicated, it is quite simple. Each item in my model is scored on a 10-point scale, with 10 being the largest amount and 1 being extremely low and 0 nothing. The full model explaining how to arrive at the "O," "r," "g" and "a" scores is:

$$S = .40L[(r_1 + r_2 + r_3 + r_4) \times b \div 4] + .25O[(.30c + .25p + .15n + .10v + .10s + .10f) - l] + .20V[(g_1 + g_2 + g_3 + g_4) \times p \div 4] + .15E[(a_1 + a_2 + a_3 + a_4) \times w \div 4]$$

where:

S = (Long-Lasting, True, Authentic and/or Sustainable) Success – scored on a 0–100-point scale (i.e., 90–100 = A; 80–89 = B; 70–79 = C)

L = love/gratitude/giving/passion for all four areas – *physiology, psychology, sociology, and philosophy*

r_1 = physiological resources/skills/traits (including health, clothing, grooming, attractiveness, talent, "deliberate" work and perceived performance; anything physical that has value)

r_2 = psychological resources/skills/traits (including reading, education, initiative, imagination, self-confidence, enthusiasm, humor, creativity, "flow," learning, ambition, self-belief, grit, information processing, data analytics, positive thinking, self-discipline, communication and problem-solving skills; anything psychological that has value)

r_3 = sociological resources/skills/traits (including relationships, social connections, networks, mentors, initial support, popularity, helping others succeed, providing value to others, doing more than paid for; anything sociological that has value)

r_4 = philosophical resources/skills/traits (including purpose, "calling," gratitude, philanthropy, belief in a higher power, faith, beliefs, ethics, morals, enjoyment of life, leaving a legacy; anything philosophical that has value)

Note: money (financial resources or access to) and time (the only variable that is totally equal for everybody and including "quiet" time) are embedded in each of the four areas

b = balance (the holistic combination of resources/skills and achieving synergy)

O = potential value (quality) of an opportunity or idea; recognizing and seizing opportunities and/or experiences

c = scalability – 30 percent of the "O" score; no idea or opportunity can be very successful without a high ability to scale; a scalable idea or opportunity has the capacity to quickly and significantly increase production to meet demand without sacrificing quality and achieve economies of scale.

p = passion or purpose – this variable repeatedly shows up as significant not only in the idea but in all areas of the formula; this variable is equal to 25 percent of the "O" score and may be defined as (1) what you are most passionate about, (2) your life's purpose, vision, or calling, (3) what gives you "bliss," (4) what puts you in a state of "flow," or (5) "the great work of your life." No idea can be very successful without a person having a high level of passion for it.

n = need – 15 percent of the "O" score; always ask if the idea is practical, useable (by a significant target market or audience), marketable, stable, sticky (ability to become a habit, trend or go viral).

v = price/value – 10 percent of the "O" score; price is the amount paid for acquiring any product, service, idea or experience and it is not always money. Value is the utility of a good or service for a target customer.

s = previous success(es) – 10 percent of the "O" score; Many researchers maintain that the age-old adage that "success breeds success" is true. In sports, for instance, this theory is quite widespread because it does seem to work. While it seems reasonable that a first success (i.e., winning a game) would naturally lead to more successes, this theory does not explain how to get the initial success. It also doesn't explain why many times a sports team is predicted to win by a large margin and ends up losing. Nevertheless, there exists empirical research that supports this theory.

f = previous failure(s) – 10 percent of the "O" score; There is also scientific proof that previous failures at implementing ideas or opportunities may be just as important as a string of successes.

l = luck – This percentage is subtracted from the summation of the five variables above. The definition of luck is success due to chance rather than through one's own actions.

"IT'S ALWAYS DARKEST BEFORE THE DAWN"

V = visualization of having already achieved goals (feeling that you have already received)

g_1 = physiological goals

g_2 = psychological goals

g_3 = sociological goals

g_4 = philosophical goals

p = persistence for achieving your SMART goals

E = execution of actions is required to achieve your stated goals/intentions/promises

a_1 = actions for achieving physiological goals

a_2 = actions for achieving psychological goals

a_3 = actions for achieving sociological goals

a_4 = actions for achieving philosophical goals

w = level of willingness to take risks, overcome adversities, persist (not quit) and do whatever it takes to succeed (includes "grit"—the combination of passion and perseverance and exchange or choice—what you are willing to give up (or what "price" will you pay, not always money)

It should be noted that my formula is not perfect and following it will not guarantee success for all people. Nevertheless, I believe it will work for many more people than any previous or current formula. I think of it like baking bread or building a house, there will be failure unless all the ingredients are accurately put together. My formula can result in the achievement of any desire, including fame, prestige, and/or great wealth. However, it is hoped that the formula will be utilized for authentic or true success, which is what is deeply meaningful to you, what you genuinely care about, and what integrates your values.

My formula incorporates 10 of the 11 theories identified in Chapter 2 that have proven to be able to predict and/or explain personal success (or failure) to some degree. These theories are: (1) life-balance, (2) trait, (3) luck (happy accidents), (4) resource management, (5) exchange, (6) goal, (7) choice (similar to willingness to do whatever it takes to succeed), (8) expectancy (similar to willingness to do whatever it takes to succeed), (9) least action (a part of willingness to do whatever it takes to succeed), and (10) game (giving and receiving). My final formula did not include genetic theory since research shows that a person's DNA has but a minimal effect on success achievement and might not be measurable.

Finally, my formula does not contain the "law of attraction" theory or manifestation popularized by Byrne's *The Secret*. I love the concepts of the law of attraction ("like attracts like," and all you have to do is send out a message to the "universe") and manifesting (your dreams, goals, intentions or aspirations can be achieved just by believing). I wish so much that both were true. However, there is just not enough empirical evidence that these concepts work. Perhaps science hasn't caught up with reality yet! There is a joke about a woman utilizing the "secret" to manifest the perfect parking spot directly in front of a store, and she got it on her 16th or 60th trip (depending on the version of the story) around the block!

Tim Denning writes, "Success isn't complicated. All you need is a formula to follow.... Formulas make the future crystal clear. The only unknown is how big your success will be when you follow the formula." You now have a formula!

CHAPTER 6

WHAT'S LOVE GOT TO DO WITH IT?

Love/Gratitude, the Most Important Trait Hidden in Plain Sight—and Other Success Variables

$$S = .40L[(r_1 + r_2 + r_3 + r_4) \, X \, b \div 4]$$
$$+ .25O[(.30c + .25p + .15n + .10v + .10s + .10f) - 1]$$

$$+ .20V[(g_1 + g_2 + g_3 + g_4) \, X \, p \div 4]$$
$$+ .15E[(a_1 + a_2 + a_3 + a_4) \, X \, w \div 4]$$

L = love/gratitude/giving/passion

r_1 = physiological resources/skills/traits

r_2 = psychological resources/skills/traits

r_3 = sociological resources/skills/traits

r_4 = philosophical resources/skills/traits

b = balance

Once a woman came out of her house and saw three elderly men with long white beards sitting in her front yard. She did not recognize them. She said, "I don't think I know you, but you must be hungry. Please come in and have something to eat."

"We do not go into a house together," they replied. One of the old men explained: "His name is Wealth," he said pointing to one of his friends, and said pointing to another one, "He is Success, and I am Love." Then he added, "Now go in and discuss with your husband which one of us you want in your home."

The woman went in and told her husband what was said. Her husband was overjoyed. "How nice!!" he said. "Since that is the case, let us invite Wealth. Let him come and fill our home with wealth!"

His wife disagreed. "My dear, why don't we invite Success?" Their daughter was listening from the other corner of the house. She jumped in with her own suggestion: "Would it not be better to invite Love? Our home will then be filled with love!" "Let us heed our daughter's advice," said the husband to his wife. "Go out and invite Love to be our guest."

The woman went out and asked the men, "Love, please come in and be our guest." Love got up and started walking toward the house. The other two men also got up and followed him. Surprised, the woman asked Wealth and Success: "I only invited Love. Why are you coming in?"

The men replied together: "If you had invited Wealth or Success, the other two of us would've stayed out, but since you invited Love, wherever he goes, we go with him. Wherever there is Love, there is also Wealth and Success!"

While the origin of this story is unknown and there are numerous versions, including one with a fourth elderly man (Happiness), the moral is always the same—if your focus is on success or wealth or both, the chances of experiencing or developing *love* for yourself or others is small. However, if your focus is on love, the chance of being successful and/or wealthy (though not necessarily financially) increases dramatically! You probably know of people who have achieved a great deal of money, power, and/or fame (what many people deem as success) who are very unhappy. Therefore, the authentically successful person should first seek love.

The concept of "love" is considered by many scientists to be soft, fuzzy, or mushy, and I resisted putting it in my success model. However, time and time again love showed up as a significant variable in my formula for true, authentic, or lasting success. During the first couple weeks of the Fall 2022 semester, while I was teaching an honors course on the science of success, my students and I debated whether love could be considered a trait for authentic success. I kept dismissing it as a worthwhile trait since I didn't think the scientific evidence was sufficient. That was until I had a eureka moment while watching college football games on TV.

I observed that virtually every time a winning team's quarterback, star player, or coach was interviewed after the game, he said something about loving his teammates/players, coaches, university, and/or the fans. Week after week, I watched as the teams that won said essentially the same thing about love during their interviews. Thereafter, I began to research intensely the concept of love while continuing my experiment of listening to and recording the responses from winning teams' players and coaches. I was astonished at what I found in only two weeks. The teams that were losing—though they had substantial talent and skilled players—never (or rarely) spoke of love.

Moreover, I began to see love being written about in many places. For example, the 1996 book *NUTS! Southwest Airlines' Crazy Recipe for Business and Personal Success* by Kevin and Jackie Freiberg has an entire chapter on love (Chapter 16, "Luv—More Than Just a Ticker Symbol").

There is an excellent example of love in the 1950 book *Three Minutes a Day: Christopher Thoughts for Daily Living that have Already Inspired Millions* by James Keller titled "Ready for the Worst":

> A doctor tells this story of an eight-year-old boy whose sister was dying of a disease from which the boy himself had recovered some time before. Realizing that only a transfusion of her brother's blood would save the little girl, the doctor asked the boy: "Would you like to give your blood to your sister?" The child hesitated for a moment; his eyes wide with fear. Then, finally, he said: "Sure, Doctor, I'll do it." Only later, after the transfusion was completed, did the boy ask hesitantly, "Say, Doctor, when do I die?" Then the doctor understood the momentary hesitation and fear. It had taken the boy that long to decide to sacrifice his life for his sister.

That is love, my friend!

Dale Carnegie, in his 1937 book *How to Win Friends and Influence People*, shares the following:

> Did you ever stop to think that a dog is the only animal that doesn't have to work for a living? A hen has to lay eggs, a cow has to give milk…. But a dog makes his living by giving you nothing but love.
>
> When I [Carnegie] was five years old, my father bought a little yellow-haired pup for fifty cents…. Every afternoon about four-thirty, he would sit in the front yard with his beautiful eyes staring steadfastly at the path, and as soon as he heard my voice or saw me swinging my dinner pail through the buck brush, he was off like a shot, racing breathlessly up the hill to greet me with leaps of joy and barks of sheer ecstasy.

That is love!

Grief is an expression of love (love lost) that can also contribute to success. (It can also do the opposite, depending on whether you use it to create something good or torture yourself with it.) Eric Clapton endured unimaginable horror and suffering when his four-year-old son Connor fell to his death from the window of a Manhattan apartment building. In their 1998 book *All You Need is Love and 99 Other Life Lessons from Classic Rock Songs*, Pete Fornatale and Bill Ayres write: "Working out some of his grief through his music, Clapton wrote a

WHAT'S LOVE GOT TO DO WITH IT? | 195

poignant song about Conner called 'Tears in Heaven,' proving once again that great art can emerge from total tragedy. 'Tears in Heaven' won three Grammys in 1993—song of the year, record of the year, and best male pop vocal performance."

In addition, Fornatale and Ayres write: "All your money and fame won't help you now, but your faith and creativity will. Eric Clapton had struggled with the gift and challenge of faith all his life…. Now he used his songwriting talent to tap into the reservoir of faith that is always there if we are open to it. The result was a number-one hit but, more important[ly], a major step in the healing journey for Clapton and his family. It also wound up being a wonderful gift to thousands of other parents who have lost children to death."

And to people like me who have lost a loved one—in my case, my father. I was living three and a half hours away from my parents' home when my father died. I didn't get the call until hours later, but I immediately packed and drove home. During the drive, many times the song "Tears in Heaven" played on the car radio.

The authors go on to say: "Engaging your talents and creativity [during a time of tragedy] in whatever form fits will prevent you from feeling utterly powerless and spinning off into deep depression." This is wisdom. When I got the almost certain terminal cancer diagnosis (it's been over 31 months as I edit this), I became extremely depressed (prognosis up to one year to live without treatment and up to two years—24 months—with treatment). But even then, I was writing this book.

By continuing to write (even though there were/are days I didn't/don't feel well enough to get out of bed or up from

196 | THE SUCCESS PYRAMID

the recliner), I have noticed that I have become less depressed. Every morning, I have something to look forward to doing! Tom Bodett is credited with saying, "They say a person needs just three things to be truly happy [successful] in this world: someone to love, something to do, and something to hope for." Writing this book has and continues to be a "labor of love." And I hope this book will honor my father's memory by helping many people achieve the success they have desired but has eluded them.

Kaleel Jamison (who died of breast cancer at age 53 in 1985) in her book *The Nibble Theory and the Kernel of Power: A Book about Leadership, Self-empowerment, and Personal Growth* gives an example of love working like a candle: "When you give away some of the light from the [your] candle, by lighting another person's candle, there isn't less light because you've given some away, there's more." You can watch a video about her titled "She Made a Difference" at https://www.youtube.com/watch?v=qOpofBeL1og.

In his lifetime, John Marks Templeton wrote a lot of books, and he wrote a great deal about love. In this quote, Templeton echoes Jamison:

> As we release love energy, a chain reaction takes place. When it flows through us, it changes and enlarges us. It opens our hearts which were closed due to bitterness. We are flooded with acceptance and joy. We begin to love ourselves and don't need to search for it outside ourselves. This love energy is a healing balm. It has no perception of good or evil. It must be a continuous

process of filling ourselves and letting it out to
others.... It is like a spark in an engine. We can't
stop it from flowing to others.... Love gives and
gives without diminution of supply.

Love, like any skill, must be practiced. I think of the Olympic athletes who practice many hours every day for many years and then win or lose a medal by fractions of a second. They must love their sport! Research clearly shows that you must love what you do (for a living) and love others if you want to be truly successful in life. Templeton writes:

To develop it [love], we must practice until
it becomes our second nature—as natural as
breathing. It is a deliberate choice we can make
right now.... It is like the exercise program in
which we begin with simpler exercises and progressively do more as our strength increases. The
reward is feeling good and improving our ability.
With love, we feel good about ourselves and others—two important components of a happy life.

With love as the most important trait for success, I thought I had discovered something unique until I read Jim Tressel's 2008 book *The Winners Manual for the Game of Life*. Tressel devotes an entire chapter to "love" and how utilizing it had won his teams five national titles! Like the life balance model, I developed the love concept independently and was amazed to discover that it was already known (though very few of the most well-known success writers mention it). Tressel writes, "We can have all the makings of a championship team, all the coaching talent in the world, and all the top recruits from around the country, but without the hidden component of love and concern for our fellow team members, we're going to come up short."

Tressel writes that "From the moment we're born to the moment we die, life is about relationships." Moreover, Tressel defined love as "the deep sense of commitment that each player has for every other player; the feeling of commitment that each player has for every coach—and vice versa; and the feeling of commitment that each coach has for every other coach. If each of these three relationships is not based on love, the team will not achieve its full potential." Tressel summarizes, "Those feelings—those commitments—must then be followed up with commensurate *action*."

Tressel credits Dr. Patrick "Doc" Spurgeon, a retired English professor from Georgia Southern University who died June 23, 2022, at age 92, with having a great deal of influence on his five national championships. Tressel writes, "He [Doc Spurgeon] has told my players and me time and again that in order to be champions, every team needs two basic components: *love* and *discipline*. And if we have love, the discipline will follow, because players who love each other don't want to let the team down."

A man who had been watching Ohio State games on TV told Doc, "They think you win tough games with talent. You don't win tough games with talent. You win tough games with toughness. And the way you get tough is through love." Tressel writes, "Love has a way of making unexpected things happen.

Love can transform a team of players with less than stellar talent into a tightly knit group that can perform above its level of ability." Could Tressel be referring to synergy, which is a large component of my success model?

Tressel echoed Templeton: "The wonderful thing about showing genuine concern for other people is that the giver gains as much as the receiver, if not more. There is a by-product of love for both giver and receiver that can't be quantified on a spreadsheet." But Tressel admits that "Loving others is not easy. You have to make time for it in your busy schedule. It has to be an intentional part of your plan, one that you put in writing. And love's schedule is not always convenient. It's easy to say you want to show love, but it's something else to truly commit yourself to doing it."

Personally, I try to be friendly (show love) to everyone I meet—from the lowest to the highest. Perhaps it is easier for me since I was born into a community that knew poverty. I think this old saying is true: "Be nice to people on the way up because you are going to meet them on the way down!"

Recently, I discovered that *The Secret* (sold over 35 million copies) author Rhonda Byrne had in 2010 published the book *The Power* (about love, and sold over 4 million copies) and in 2012 the book *The Magic* (about gratitude, sold over 1 million copies). My research shows that love and gratitude are one and the same. Byrne writes in the Foreword: "In *The Power* you will come to understand that all it takes is just one thing to change your relationships, money, health, happiness, career, and your entire life." And that one thing is unconditional love! Byrne goes on to write, "Without exception, every person who has a great life used *love* to achieve it.... Love is the cause of *everything* positive and good."

Byrne askes the question: "Why aren't you filled with joy every day? The answer is: because you have a choice (Ah, Choice Theory). You have a choice whether to love and harness the positive force—or not." Moreover, Byrne writes, "Every action of *giving* creates an opposite action of *receiving* and what you receive is always equal to what you've given. Whatever you give out in life must return to you.... It's impossible to have a great life without love." Finally, Byrne writes, "To change your life, all you have to do is tip the scales by giving 51 percent love through your good thoughts and good feelings. It is what you feel *today* that matters, because it is the *only* thing that determines your future."

The Power isn't the only book about the importance of love in creating success. There is actually a 2020 book titled *Love: The Secret to Success* by Mark Hankins. It is a Christian book and does not contain much science. However, there was a lot of wisdom in it. Another example is Henry Drummond's book *The Greatest Thing in the World,* which was his interpretation of the 13th chapter of Second Corinthians—the "love chapter." While written in 1956 (before I was born), this small book (61 pages) had sold over a million copies by the time my edition came out (fourth printing, 1970)! Drummond argues that there are nine vital ingredients of love: (1) patience, (2) kindness, (3) humility, (4) generosity, (5) courtesy, (6) unselfishness, (7) good temper, (8) guilelessness, and (9) sincerity. These are all qualities of a successful person we have already determined. Drummond wrote that these qualities/ingredients can be learned, but only through constant practice in daily life.

Drummond tells stories of various individuals who built a legacy on love, with the central message that "there is no happiness in having and getting anything, but only in giving.... Half the world is on the wrong scent in pursuit of happiness [success]. They think it consists in having and getting, and in being served by others. It consists in giving, and in serving others."

Along the same lines, Mother Teresa said that the most "powerful" weapons on earth are love and prayer and that to heal troubled relationships just tell people that you love them. She writes, "Happiness [success] is a by-product of love. Constant, unconditional love will communicate itself to even the most badly abused. Love is the one power that eventually can cut through all obstacles."

French priest and philosopher Pierre Teilhard de Chardin said, "Someday, after we have mastered the winds, the waves, the tides and gravity, we shall harness the energies of Love. Then, for the second time in the history, man will have discovered fire."

The quote, "Love yourself by being the very best you can possibly be" has been attributed to the South Korean music group BTS, specifically their leader, Kim Namjoon (RM), who frequently promotes self-love and personal growth messages through their music and interviews.

We all want love and companionship, and both are essential for authentic success. However, it is a universal law that you must love first. Further, you must become non-judgmental for your love to begin.

In summary, you might need more than love to succeed, but love certainly should be the bedrock out of which the other success traits are shaped.

HAVING A GREAT IDEA/ OPPORTUNITY IS NOT ENOUGH

$$S = .40L[(r_1 + r_2 + r_3 + r_4) \times b \div 4]$$
$$+ .25O[(.30c + .25p + .15n + .10v + .10s + .10f) - l]$$
$$+ .20V[(g_1 + g_2 + g_3 + g_4) \times p \div 4]$$
$$+ .15E[(a_1 + a_2 + a_3 + a_4) \times w \div 4]$$

O = potential value (quality) of an opportunity or idea

c = scalability

p = passion or purpose

n = need

v = price/value

s = previous success(es)

f = previous failure(s)

l = luck

A good idea/opportunity is important, but alone isn't enough for success. W. A. Ward said "Opportunities are like sunrises. If you wait too long, you miss them." And I have certainly missed a lot of great opportunities. For example, I recently had the opportunity to purchase a property on which

I could have earned a quick $100,000. However, I got frustrated about a minor issue with the contract and decided not to take the deal. While missed opportunities have happened to me quite a bit, I have jumped on a few great opportunities that have made money and/or achieved a goal! Though the sun rises every morning, opportunities or great ideas don't come that often. That's why when you find them, you should grab them immediately. Opportunities are fleeting and will pass you by if you wait too long to act.

There is a story about a visitor to a sculptor's studio who was shown many "gods." One whose face was concealed by hair and had wings on its feet intrigued the visitor. "What is its name?" asked the visitor. "Opportunity," replied the sculptor. "Why is its face hidden?" asked the visitor. "Because men [people] seldom know him when he comes to them." The visitor then asked, "Why has he wings on his feet?" The sculptor answered, "Because he is soon gone, and once gone, cannot be overtaken."

There is a quote (or an Arabian proverb) that you should really heed: "Four things do not come back: the spoken word, the sped arrow, time past, the neglected opportunity." This quote is widely attributed to science fiction author Ted Chiang, but some sources argue that Omar Ibn Al-Halif should be credited with saying it first.

You have probably regretted things you have said to or about others (usually in the heat of the moment) or things you have done in your past. But you likely most regret what you didn't say or do! Nevertheless, you must forgive yourself and, if appropriate, ask forgiveness from others. But most importantly, you must never neglect an opportunity. You never know when a specific opportunity will change your life for the better!

Richard Branson in a blog post on "How to Spot an Opportunity" says that opportunities do not always come at the perfect time. So, you must be ready to seize them when the chance presents itself. There is no point in waiting to act. If you hesitate, they will likely disappear. Branson advises to "put yourself in the right mindset to spot opportunities."

This is one reason why I really liked Napoleon Hill's "The Habit of Saving" principle that he included in his first two books (1928 and 1930) but not in *Think and Grow Rich* (1937). I've always been a "saver" (perhaps because I hate to pay interest). So I always have had the financial resources (nest egg) to take advantage of opportunities that presented themselves unexpectedly. Hill writes "[I]t may be, and perhaps is true, that money is not success, but unless you have it or can command its use, you will not get far, no matter what might be your definite chief aim." Hill was clear that the amount saved was *not* important—the saving had to be "regular and systematic." Further, Hill writes, "the habit of saving adds something to the other qualities essential for success which can be had in no other way."

Branson quoted columnist Ann Landers, who wrote, "Opportunities are usually disguised as hard work, so most people don't recognize them." Ironically, hard work is the key to taking advantage of opportunities. If you put in the time, effort, and commitment, you'll open many doors for yourself. It's only a matter of noticing opportunities and acting upon them.

Einstein said, "In the middle of difficulty lies opportunity." I believe Einstein meant that there are numerous opportunities available even during the worst of times, but most people will not recognize them or even be looking for them. Einstein also said, "Adversity introduces a man [person] to himself [or herself]." I think he meant that people show their real selves when faced with adversity and that they don't know how they will react or behave until then.

Opportunities don't have to be spectacular in appearance to be successful. Indeed, often the mundane leads to great success. Orison Swett Marden, in his book *Pushing to the Front,* writes, "Don't wait for extraordinary opportunities. *Seize common occasions and make them great."* *Pushing to The Front* was originally published in 1894. The book was revised and expanded into a two-volume work in 1911. At 70 chapters and nearly 900 pages, it is considered an encyclopedia of success. In the 2006 book *212° The Extra Degree,* authors Sam Parker and Mac Anderson argue that many opportunities have been missed because people were not aware of the possibilities that would occur if they applied a small amount of effort beyond what they normally would.

Sometimes the best opportunities are the "scrap" or something someone has given up on prematurely. The opportunity might simply need some improvement—perhaps only minor—to turn into success. The 2009 book *Three Feet from Gold: Turn Your Obstacles into Opportunities!* by Sharon L. Lechter and Greg S. Reid took its title from the story shared earlier in this book—told by Napoleon Hill in *Think and Grow Rich*—about the man who sold his gold mine when it seemingly stopped yielding gold to another man, who discovered that the major vein picked up again just three feet away where it had appeared to stop. The secret? Sometimes our success is closer than we think!

Audrey Menen said, "The essence of success is that it is never necessary to think of a new idea oneself. It is far better to wait until somebody else does it and then to copy him in every detail, except his mistakes." During 44 years of teaching marketing at the university level, I often encouraged my students to be first to be second (on the market)! That way the initial problems (and there are always problems) with the innovation can be corrected.

A lack of opportunities is not an excuse. Good opportunities are everywhere, waiting to be discovered. Some people get more opportunities than others, or so it seems (though it may be that some people are better at "recognizing" opportunities). It is equally true that all have at least one great opportunity at some time in life, and failure is due not to the lack of an opportunity but to not taking advantage of it. I've been unable to determine who said, "There is nobody whom Fortune does not visit once in his life, but when she finds he is not ready to receive her, she goes in at the door and out at the window." But the quote contains a secret—be persistent in looking for opportunities and be prepared to take advantage of opportunities when they present. For more on this, see John Martin's book *Power of Persistence*.

Some people argue that getting opportunities is largely a matter of accident, luck, or being in the right place at the right time. While this may be true in some cases, it is very possible to "make" opportunities. I've been unable to determine who said, "What we call a turning-point is simply an occasion which sums up and brings to a result previous training. Accidental circumstances [opportunities] are nothing except to men [people] who have been trained to take advantage of them. We are

WHAT'S LOVE GOT TO DO WITH IT? | 207

expecting mastery without apprenticeship, knowledge without study, and riches by credit." So, train yourself to always be on the lookout for "great" opportunities.

So, what makes for a potential high value idea/opportunity? First, you must be (1) passionate about it and it must be connected to (2) your life's purpose, vision or calling, (3) what gives you "bliss," (4) what puts you in a state of "flow," and/or (5) "the great work of your life." No idea can be very successful if you do not have a high level of passion for it. I advise those who have great ideas (or opportunities) for which they personally are not super passionate about but know have value should either (1) sell the idea to someone who is passionate about it, (2) trade it, (3) lease it, or (4) give it away (to a non-profit or to a supplier). The idea will never be successful if a passionless person attempts to implement it. Refer back to my formula— the highest "O" score possible with no passion is 75!

Second, it must be "scalable." A scalable idea or opportunity has the capacity to quickly and significantly increase production to meet demand without sacrificing quality and achieve economies of scale. This is as true for personal ideas as for business opportunities.

Third, there must be a demonstrated need for the "idea." Always ask if your idea is practical, useable (by a significant target market or audience), marketable, stable, and sticky (ability to become a habit, trend, or to go viral).

Fourth, it must be able to be value priced. Remember that price is the amount paid for acquiring any product, service, idea, or experience and it is not always money. Value is the utility of a good or service for a target customer or audience.

Fifth, previous success(es) must be considered. Many researchers maintain that the age-old adage that "success breeds success" and the old French proverb "nothing succeeds like success" are true and there exists empirical research that supports both.

Sixth, previous failure(s) must be examined. There is also scientific proof that previous failures at implementing ideas or opportunities may be just as important as a string of successes. James Sharp writes, "It is not every calamity that is a curse, and early adversity is often a blessing. Surmounted difficulties not only teach but hearten us in our future struggles."

Finally, "luck" is to be subtracted from the sum of these six variables. The definition of luck is success due to chance rather than through your own actions. Like genetics or predestination theories, some researchers believe you become successful because you are lucky enough to be born in a particular place and/or time, get 10,000 hours of practice, happen to be in the "right place at the right time," or lucky enough to have somebody backing you (a devoted family member or significant other, rich person, great mentor or coach). For example, success at playing chess is almost all pure skill, while winning at roulette (or a slot machine) is almost all pure luck. Success in the stock market is mostly luck, too. It must be remembered, however, that there is no way to place every activity on the luck-skill continuum precisely; these percentages are to be used only to help you discover better opportunities or make better decisions.

Other researchers argue that you make your own luck or somehow (whether genetically or learned) are better able to see the potential in ideas or opportunities when presented to you. According to Michael J. Mauboussin's book *The Success Equation*, "Much of what we experience in life results from a combination of skill and luck.... The trick, of course, is figuring out just how many of our successes (and failures) can be attributed to each—and how we can learn to tell the difference *ahead of time*." Mauboussin continues, "In most domains of life, skill and luck seem hopelessly entangled. Different levels of skill and varying degrees of good and bad luck are the realities that shape our lives—yet few of us are adept at accurately distinguishing between the two. Imagine what we could accomplish if we were able to tease out these two threads, examine them, and use the resulting knowledge to make better decisions."

Research suggests after you subtract luck, you should add a score for humor. Here is a humorous example of luck: "In the mid-1970s, a man hunted for a lottery ticket with the last two digits ending in 48 [apparently you couldn't select your own numbers like you can today]. He found a ticket, bought it, and then won the lottery. When asked why he was intent on finding that number, he replied, 'I dreamed of the number 7 for seven straight nights. And 7 times 7 is 48.'" (From Stanley Meisler, "First in 1763: Spain Lottery—Not Even a War Stops It," *Los Angeles Times*, December 30, 1977, A5.)

There is scientific evidence from numerous clinical trials that humor can enhance success and be healing. Charles and Frances Hunter wrote a 2003 book titled *Healing Through Humor*. The authors discussed scientific research regarding what happens to your body when you laugh. It includes the fact that your body releases endorphins (natural pain killers) and you produce more immune cells (which can be very beneficial to cancer patients). Dr. Francisco Contreras, a surgical oncologist, writes in the Foreword:

> I have often said that fear is the stronghold of cancer [and perhaps the reason success eludes so many people]. Cancer is an opportunistic disease. Fear and other negative emotions are detrimental to the immune system. Depression and anxiety are open invitations for cancer to have its way with a patient. When we are able to help a person smile and laugh, I know that we increase the possibility of recovery markedly. One of my goals is to help patients get to a place where they can stare cancer right in the eyes and say, "You cannot rob my joy." For me, laughter therapy is not a warm fuzzy activity that is a nice service to offer patients if time allows. It is an essential part of our treatment program.

The authors quoted Dr. Contreras in the Preface: "One bout of anger will diminish the efficiency of your immune system for six hours, but one good laugh will increase the efficiency of your immune system for twenty-four hours."

Humor—and attitude in general—can affect the way you identify (or miss) opportunities. As John C. Maxwell, in his 2000 book *Success: One Day at a Time*, writes:

1. The more motivated you are, the more you will recognize opportunities

2. Your attitude will determine your recognizing great opportunities

3. Today is the best day for an opportunity—"someday" should *not* be on your calendar

4. Opportunities are the result of pluck, not luck

5. Opportunities don't present themselves in ideal circumstances, already discussed

6. Opportunity without commitment [passion] will be lost [already discussed]

7. Opportunity is birthed out of problems [already discussed]

8. Opportunities either multiply or disappear [already discussed]

9. Opportunities must be nourished if they are to survive. [Maxwell quoted Peter Drucker, "Feed an opportunity; starve a problem."]

When plugged into the pyramid model, the following was empirically found to be significant for discovering opportunities.

For physiology, you can increase the likelihood of discovering new opportunities by:

1. Taking people out for coffee or a meal (especially connections outside your regular "circle" or network)

2. Exercising with "new" people (or going to a large gym)

3. Dressing for success, emulating people whose clothes would look good on you, and wearing really good shoes

4. Always being well groomed

5. Doing activities to reduce physical stress

6. Getting sufficient sleep (rest)

7. Smiling and laughing a lot

For psychology, you should always be looking for high potential opportunities by being:

1. Proactive through continually evaluating information and ideas to which you are exposed

2. Reading good books

3. Noticing market gaps in existing products, services, or situations

4. Identifying unmet needs (or desires)

5. Making good choices

6. Being creative

7. Not worrying or being fearful

8. Being enthusiastic and developing positive habits

The late Charlie "Tremendous" Jones in his two million-plus bestselling book *Life is Tremendous* (1968) says, "You will be the same person in five years as you are today except for the people you meet and the books you read."

For sociology, scientific research suggests that opportunity identification can be achieved by:

1. Showing love to everyone you come in contact with (the most important scientific finding)

2. Showing gratitude for everything you receive or have (including family and friends) and not being envious of what others have

3. Developing a wide network to expose yourself to novel information and innovative opportunities

4. Cultivating people in your network from diverse backgrounds as most people find great jobs, for example, not by talking with close friends or responding to ads but through "distant" connections

5. Actively participating in community, fraternal, and other organizations

6. Developing no need for power, to control others, to criticize, or to play roles

7. Practicing reciprocity—all relationships reflect your relationship with yourself

Esther Perel said, "The quality of your life ultimately depends on the quality of your relationships." She also said that relationships reflect your sense of decency, your ability to think of others, and your generosity. You should minimize the faults in others and magnify their virtues. While you influence every person you encounter, you don't need to seek the approval of others.

For philosophy, scientific research indicates that you can find significant opportunities by:

1. Discovering your purpose (i.e., through your church, synagogue, or mosque)

2. Being kind and nonjudgmental

3. Practicing spiritual activities, meditation, experiencing silence, or observing quiet time

4. Embracing simplicity

In summary, the scientific findings regarding opportunities are:

1. Opportunities are everywhere and occur frequently, and failure is not due to the lack of opportunities but to not being persistent in recognizing them.

2. Many people don't have the resources saved or available to them to take advantage of a great opportunity, especially when presented during difficult or inconvenient times.

3. Great opportunities are usually disguised as "hard work" or "mundane," and many people neglect them even when they need only a slight adjustment to become exceedingly successful.

4. The components of a great opportunity are well known—add passion, scalability, need (or desire), value price, previous success (and failure), and humor and subtract luck.

BEING ABLE TO VISUALIZE COMPLETION OF GOALS IS NOT ENOUGH

$$S = .40L[(r_1 + r_2 + r_3 + r_4) \, X \, b \div 4]$$
$$+ .25O[(.30c + .25p + .15n + .10v + .10s + .10f) - l]$$

$$+ .20V[(g_1 + g_2 + g_3 + g_4) \, X \, e \div 4]$$
$$+ .15E[(a_1 + a_2 + a_3 + a_4) \, X \, w \div 4]$$

V = visualization of having already achieved goals

g_1 = physiological goals

g_2 = psychological goals

g_3 = sociological goals

g_4 = philosophical goals

e = persistence for achieving your SMART goals

The goal-setting theory has been defined as what you are trying to accomplish or the object or aim of an action. Goal setting is the process of establishing specific and effective targets for task performance that provide a positive influence. Research also shows that a specific high goal leads to even higher performance than urging people to do their best. Andril Sedniev in his 2018 book *Insane Success for Lazy People* writes,

"There is a direct relationship between everything you achieve in life and how clearly you specify your goals, because the clarity of your goals impacts the preciseness and effectiveness of your actions." Moreover, Sedniev writes, "Knowing clearly how your dream life looks is the most important step towards making your dream life a reality."

While having goals is important for success, it alone is not enough. Having SMART goals is essential, however. As mentioned previously, SMART is a mnemonic acronym giving criteria to guide in the setting of goals and objectives for better results especially in personal development (success). The letters "S" and "M" generally mean "specific" and "measurable." Possibly the most common version has the remaining letters referring to "achievable" (or attainable), "relevant," and "time bound." I'm not a big fan of mnemonic acronyms because so many are contrived to form clever words. However, I'll make an exception for SMART goals since it is rooted in scientific research.

The principal advantage of SMART objectives is to give a clear roadmap. You will have a clear understanding of what you need to take action on, and you will be able to evaluate the outcome based on defined criteria. Ideally, each objective should be:

- *Specific* – Target a specific area for improvement. Can also be "strategic," but "specific" is the best term.

- *Measurable* – Quantify or at least suggest an indicator of progress. Can also be "motivating," but "measurable" is the best term.

- *Achievable* – Being action-oriented or ambitious. Can also be "attainable," but "achievable" is the best term.

- *Relevant* – What results can realistically be achieved given available resources. Can also be "realistic," "reasonable" or "results-based," but "relevant" is the best term since it implies that the goal is in line with your purpose, mission, vision, or calling.

- *Time-bound* – When the result(s) can be achieved. Can also be "trackable," "time/cost limited," "time sensitive," or "testable," but "time-bound" is the best term.

In addition to the five SMART features, your goal(s) should also be *collaborative* since very little is accomplished without the help of others. Moreover, your goal(s) should be *positively stated* and *ethical* and designed to do *no harm to others.* Finally, your goal(s) should be of *high quality, believable,* and those in which *you are completely committed.*

Peter Drucker said that "if you have more than five goals, you have none." Drucker's point was that goals are intended to focus you and should include only the most important. Another researcher said that you should concentrate on one goal at a time. However, the research is not clear on this, and I have always had the opinion that you can and should work on several goals at the same time—especially one or two from each of the four sides of the pyramid. Recall Maslow never intended for his pyramid to be a hierarchy since this would imply you would have to satisfy (at least minimally) lower-level goals before you could work on higher-level ones.

Bill Bartmann is correct in that your goal(s) should be the ones you have a "burning" desire to achieve and should be challenging enough to require a lot of hard work or deliberate practice. A goal should be motivating and make you "reach" by stretching your abilities (talent) and pushing you past your comfort zone (challenge). You should have a plan for achieving these goals, and you should get regular feedback along the way. Yogi Berra said, "You've got to be careful if you don't know where you are going, because you might not get there."

One of my goals when I was in my early 20s was to become a millionaire (specific and measurable) by the time I was 30 (time-bound). I wasn't sure that this was realistic since when I graduated from college at age 21, my net worth was minus $800! Nevertheless, some real estate investments and stocks paid off and I achieved this goal by age 33 or 34. While I missed the "time-bound" feature, the goal would not have been achieved if I had not written it down and been so specific. It should be noted that my passion was college teaching (with businesses on the side), and I was working on master and doctoral degrees at the same time.

In his 1982 book *The Ultimate Secret to Getting Absolutely Everything You Want*, Mike Hernacki referred to goals as "intentions," while Bill Bartmann, in his 2006 book *Billionaire: Secrets to Success*, called goals "promises." While I love both terms, I really like the idea of a "promise." In the nine principles or "rules" for success Bartmann develops, he underscores the importance of both telling yourself you will succeed and envisioning the result when you do.

The best examples of visualizing success are probably in athletics. Research shows that setting goals can help athletes prioritize what is most important in their sport and subsequently guide daily practices by knowing what to work on.

In his 1994 book *True Success: A New Philosophy of Excellence*, Tom Morris tells a story of one of his wife's college instructors, who said, "Lots of famous and accomplished people have reported that their lives began to turn around and change for the better only when they made a list of their goals in life. In fact, I [the instructor] *guarantee* you that if you'll just write some goals down on a little piece of paper, no matter how big they are, they *will* come true." Based on my own research, this works!

With these important factors (e.g., specificity, challenge, ability, feedback, effort) applied to goals, people tend to have better performance and are more willing to face new challenges. As you can see from the above discussion, goal setting can play a significant role in enhancing people's motivation and performance. People who set specific, challenging goals and commit to these goals are more likely to try their best and persist in achieving the goals, which can lead to better performance and success.

Of course, success can come not only from achieving goals, but from failing and starting again.

Malcolm Forbes said, "Failure is success if we learn from it."

TAKING ACTION ON GOALS IS NOT ENOUGH

$$S = .40L[(r_1 + r_2 + r_3 + r_4) \times b \div 4]$$
$$+ .25O[(.30c + .25p + .15n + .10v + .10s + .10f) - 1]$$
$$+ .20V[(g_1 + g_2 + g_3 + g_4) \times p \div 4]$$
$$+ .15E[(a_1 + a_2 + a_3 + a_4) \times w \div 4]$$

E = execution of actions are required to achieve your stated goals/intentions/promises

a_1 = actions for achieving physiological goals

a_2 = actions for achieving psychological goals

a_3 = actions for achieving sociological goals

a_4 = actions for achieving philosophical goals

w = level of willingness to take risks, overcome adversities, and persist

Andril Sedniev, in his book *Insane Success for Lazy People*, writes, "The only thing you can control in life is you and your actions." Actions are required, despite some researchers suggesting that the "universe" will manifest your goals (or desires) just by letting the "universe" know you want something. There is an old story that illustrates this myth. A woman prayed every day to God to let her win the lottery and she never did. Many years later, she died. When she got to heaven, she asked God why He never answered her prayer to win the lottery. God replied, "You needed to help me out. You needed to buy a lottery ticket" [take some action]!

Taking action can be micro and/or major, but either is good as long as the action results in continuous improvement and moves you closer to achieving your goal(s). As Sedniev writes, "You are happy because of progress toward the goal—not achieving the goal."

"Small Wins" theory (see Chapter 2) suggests that seemingly insignificant minor choices (actions) can have large consequences. In *212: The Extra Degree*, Sam Parker and Mac Anderson point out that water is hot at 211° but boils at 212°—their point being that "seemingly small things can make tremendous differences." They also note that many researchers "promote methods of achieving results with little or no effort." But for many people, action is the missing ingredient and "there is even a smaller number who make the extra effort necessary to reach the desired results that were originally set to be achieved." The authors argue it is because of a lack of commitment, not desire.

Further, taking action always involves some risk, especially for "challenging" goals. Hernacki was correct when he stated you must be "willing to do whatever it takes" to achieve your goals, intentions, or promises. The key word is "willing"—often you don't have to "do" all the things you may have originally thought. Moreover, Martin was also correct in *The Power of Persistence* that you must "persist" in pursuit of your endeavors. Finally, take some action every day, even if it is only a little. Consistent progress builds toward big success.

WHAT'S LOVE GOT TO DO WITH IT? | 223

From teasing apart the major components of my new success formula, it's clear that investing in one ingredient at the expense of another will not yield desirable results. Love provides a strong foundation by generating the most productive mindset and environment for authentic success, so that when worthwhile opportunities arise, you recognize them. You also must set clear goals and visualize your success, taking action every day toward achieving them. Success truly is a science, and like a good scientist, if you measure the components effectively, study the results, and adjust accordingly—you'll build toward the reaction (success) you set out to achieve, or perhaps uncover something even greater.

CONCLUSION

OVERNIGHT SUCCESS SOMETIMES TAKES A LONG TIME

So When You Get There, Be Sure It's Authentic to You

There is an old legend, recounted in James Keller's *Three Minutes a Day*, about Aaron, a fisherman who lived on the banks of a river. As he was walking home after work daydreaming about what he would do when he became rich, he stumbled on a leather pouch filled with what he thought were small stones. Without thinking, he picked up the pouch and began throwing the pebbles into the water.

"When I am rich" he said to himself, "I'll have a large house." And he threw a stone. "I'll have servants and wine and rich food," he thought.

This continued until only one stone remained. A ray of light caused the stone to sparkle in his hand. Aaron then realized that it was a valuable gem, that he had been throwing away real riches while he daydreamed of unreal riches in the future. And he threw another stone into the river.

Like this legend, we are all guilty of wishing and dreaming about a wonderful future—someday—and without thinking, throwing away precious resources. But one thing I have told my students during the past 44 years and that science has proven: the greatest hindrance to present success (including healing, happiness) is the past too well remembered and the future too well envisioned. Of course, it is important to "plan." I am reminded of the Yiddish proverb "Man plans, God laughs." This means that human plans can frequently be upset by unforeseen circumstances. However, you should continue to plan and set goals, not dwelling on what you should have done in the past or what you are going to do "someday" in the future. My good friend Don Green, Executive Director of the Napoleon Hill Foundation, often reminds me that "Someday" is not on *any* calendar! You should make every attempt to live in the present and fully enjoy the experience.

The world's most successful people are intentional about cultivating a mindset where they can learn from the past, focus on the present, and plan for the future. In his 2004 book, *Trump: Think Like a Billionaire*, Donald J. Trump outlines his top ten ways of thinking like a billionaire. Most relevant to our present discussion is his fourth recommendation—"Have a short attention span." While some may think this would undercut one's success, focusing intensely on one matter at a time and not dwelling on it too long creates the space and intentionality to turn ideas into outcomes.

In his 1997 book *Success is a Choice*, Rick Pitino writes that every year at the beginning of their first college basketball practice, he gathers the players around him and reads to them a five-minute book titled *The Precious Present* by Spencer Johnson. Pitino's point is the past is gone and should only be used to learn from mistakes made.

An important part of this learning process is ensuring your goals build toward authentic success, rather than the appearance of success. Henry David Thoreau said, "The greatest tragedy in life is to spend your whole life fishing only to discover that it was not fish you were after." Bob Buford in his Foreword to Lloyd Reeb's book *Success to Significance: When the Pursuit of Success Isn't Enough* (2004), quotes three assertions about research on success. Two are related directly to authentic or true success. The first: "Society is undergoing a fundamental shift from 'material want' to 'meaning want,' with ever larger numbers of people reasonably secure in terms of living standards, but feeling they lack significance in their lives." The second: "new [in 2003] psychological research, which seeks to explain why some are happy and others not, suggests it in your self-interest to be forgiving, grateful, and optimistic—that these presumptively altruistic qualities are actually 'essential to personal well-being.'"

Buford goes on to write, "Nearly all well-being research supports the basic conclusion that money and material needs are only weakly associated with leading a good life. The magic number at which money decouples from happiness is far less than you might think."

To illustrate the difference between success and authentic success, there's a wonderful story titled, "The Devil Finds Work," by Mack Reynolds in *100 Great Fantasy Short Short Stories* (1984). In the story, a poet "sells" his soul which he didn't think he had or that it didn't have any value until the Devil wanted to buy it for "twenty years of whatsoever your heart desires." The poet signs the contract in blood, of course. It is such an intriguing story because it illustrates dramatically that your "heart desires" might not be your real passions. And, too, a rational person would wonder if the Devil would "keep his side of the bargain." You have sold your soul which to a religious person would be priceless. Finally, twenty years is *not* a long time—ask anyone my age (67 at the time of this writing/editing)!

I intentionally avoid mixing religion with science in this book. However, there exists scientific evidence that religious people (of all faiths, not just Christians) are happier and live longer than those who do not believe in a higher power. This is likely because their pursuit of success is inextricably bound up with their spirituality, where success is not measured by dollars but rather by the state of their soul.

My own battle with cancer has refined how I conceptualize success, further underscoring the importance of "intangibles" such as family, relationships, and influence/impact. Although I have no wife or children, and my only brother was killed in a car accident in 1997 when he was 40 years old, my mother, a sister, several nieces and nephews and several grand nieces and nephews are still living. I chose (Choice Theory) to spend what time I have left with them, though it meant I might not be "living life to the fullest."

While I did a lot of international travel beginning over 30 years ago, I did not visit all the places I wanted. Serving as a professor had one major advantage in that I almost always took the summers off and traveled (usually internationally). I used to put aside $500 a month (or $6,000 a year) for my summer travel. I was heavily criticized by friends and family members for spending money this way. While they viewed the expenditure as a waste of money, I always considered international travel as an investment and never an expense. It made me a better person.

Overall, I have become a better person because of this cancer diagnosis. I don't consider the cancer a "gift" (some patients do), though I would have most likely not completed this book or grown spiritually had I not gotten cancer. Mary Kay Ash writes in her book *Miracles Happen* that there are four kinds of people in this world: (1) those who make things happen, (2) those who watch things happen, (3) those who wonder what happened, and (4) those who don't know that *anything* happened! My final goal is to be one of those people who *make* things happen!

Above all, it's critical to take pride and pleasure in the journey toward success, realizing it's a life-long pursuit that evolves as we do. In the book *The Five Secrets You Must Discover Before You Die*, John Izzo and two colleagues interviewed over 200 people who had lived a long life and found happiness, contentment, wisdom, and meaning (or sense of purpose). These five secrets were: (1) be true to yourself, (2) leave no regrets, (3) become love, (4) live the moment, and (5) give more than you take.

These secrets need to be integrated into your life so that you know that your life matters and that you will not look back in regret. I often think of what John Greenleaf Whittier said: "Of all sad words of tongue and pen, the saddest are these, 'It might have been.'"

OVERNIGHT SUCCESS SOMETIMES TAKES A LONG TIME | 229

It is my sincere hope that the research, analysis, and resulting success formula detailed in this book helps you shape a life full of true, fulfilling, authentic success, so that your journey on earth is replete with lasting joy, gratitude, and satisfaction. Putting these principles into practice, I can say that my life has been nothing short of successful, and I wish the same for you.

> *The greatest hindrance to present success (including healing, happiness) is the past too well remembered and the future too well envisioned.*

APPENDIX A

DEFINITIONS OF SUCCESS

Some definitions of Success (in no certain order):

#	Definition	Key Words
1	Doris Lee McCoy—"a high degree of fulfillment in several areas: mental, social, physical, spiritual, and emotional."	Fulfillment, physical, mental, social/emotional, spiritual
2	Bob Proctor—"Reaching the goal is not success; success is moving toward the goal."	Progress toward goal(s)
3	Tony Robbins—"the ongoing process of striving to become more. It is the opportunity to continually grow emotionally, socially, spiritually, physiologically, intellectually, and financially while contributing in some positive way to others. The road to success is always under construction. It is a progressive course, not an end to be reached" (Unlimited Power, 1986, p. 4) and "to live your life in a way that causes you to feel a ton of pleasure and very little pain— and because of your lifestyle, have the people around you feel a lot more pleasure than they do pain."	Process, continuous process, life-balance, Pleasure for self and others

#	Definition	Key Words
4	Arianna Huffington—"To live the lives we truly want and deserve, and not just the lives we settle for, we need a Third Metric...a third measure of success that goes beyond the two metrics of money and power, and consists of four pillars: well-being, wisdom, wonder, and giving."	Money, power, well-being, wisdom, wonder, giving
5	John Wooden—"Success is peace of mind, which is a direct result of self-satisfaction in knowing you did your best to become the best you are capable of becoming."	Peace of mind, self-satisfaction, doing your best
6	Maya Angelou—"Success is liking yourself, liking what you do, and liking how you do it."	Liking self, what you do and how you do it
7	Winston Churchill—"Success is going from failure to failure without losing enthusiasm."	Failure(s), enthusiasm
8	Richard Branson—"Too many people measure how successful they are by how much money they make or the people that they associate with. In my opinion, true success should be measured by how happy you are." "The more you're actively and practically engaged, the more successful you will feel."	Happiness, being engaged
9	Deepak Chopra—"Success in life could be defined as the continued expansion of happiness and the progressive realization of worthy goals."	Expanding happiness, realizing goals
10	Thomas Edison—"Success is 1% inspiration, 99% perspiration."	Inspiration, work

#	Definition	Key Words
11	Eugene Adu-Wusu—*"Success (the opposite of failure) is the status of having achieved and accomplished an aim or objective. Being successful means the achievement of desired visions and planned goals. Furthermore, success can be a certain social status that describes a prosperous person that could also have gained fame for its favorable outcome. The dictionary describes success as the following: 'attaining wealth, prosperity and/or fame.'"*	Achieving goals (objectives), visions, fame, wealth
12	Imogen Roy—"Success without fulfillment is not success. It's failure. If you are materially successful but spiritually bankrupt, that's failure. If you have attained a 'high position' but at a detriment to your health and your relationships, that's failure. If you are 'greatly admired' but are plagued with self-loathing, that's failure. Success is simply being able to say in 10 years: I designed this life. I didn't settle for it. I didn't sacrifice."	Fulfillment, spiritual, health, being admired, life satisfaction
13	Jesse Jackson—"Success to me is being born in a poor or disadvantaged family and making something of yourself." (McCoy, p. 6)	Making something of yourself
14	Henry David Thoreau—"I learned this, at least, by my experiment: that if one advances confidently in the direction of his dreams, and endeavors to live the life which he has imagined, he will meet with a success unexpected in common hours."	Advance toward dreams, live life imagined

DEFINITIONS OF SUCCESS | 233

#	Definition	Key Words
15	Bessie Anderson Stanley—"He has achieved success who has lived well, laughed often, and loved much; Who has enjoyed the trust of pure women, the respect of intelligent men and the love of little children; Who has filled his niche and accomplished his task; Who has never lacked appreciation of Earth's beauty or failed to express it; Who has left the world better than he found it, Whether an improved poppy, a perfect poem, or a rescued soul; Who has always looked for the best in others and given them the best he had; Whose life was an inspiration; Whose memory a benediction."	Live well, laugh often, love much, enjoy trust, respect, filled niche, accomplished task, appreciate earth, leave world better than found it, look for best in others, be inspirational
16	Stephen R. Covey—"If you carefully consider what you want to be said of you in the funeral experience, you will find *your* definition of success."	What would want said at funeral
17	Albert Schweitzer—"The true meaning of success goes far beyond the common definitions of success, such as having a lot of money, being wealthy, having a lot of tangibles and earned degrees. Quite the opposite: true success in life cannot be measured with the above-named factors, but instead with the amount of people that are able to live a better and more advanced life because of what you created. This is the meaning of success. Not the trophies people are collecting in their lives."	The number of people who live better because of you

#	Definition	Key Words
18	Debasish Mridha—"True success is there when a person has the ability to lose himself or herself in the search of knowledge and wisdom by using love, joy, and gratitude. On the other hand, societal success comes from the progressive realizations of worthy goals."	Flow, love, joy, gratitude, progress toward goals
19	Brian Tracy—"Your true success in life begins only when you make the commitment to become excellent at what you do."	Excellent at what you do
20	Robert Kiyosaki—"The size of your success is measured by the strength of your desire, the size of your dream, and how you handle disappointment along the way."	Overcoming failures
21	Michael Jordan—"I've failed over and over and over again in my life—and that is why I succeed."	Learn from failures
22	James D. Maxon—"If you measure your life by what you own, the cavern of your heart will never be filled."	Success is not possessions
23	John Paul Warren—"There has never been a meaningful life built on easy street." "A true dreamer is one who knows how to navigate in the dark." "I have learned that the harder you fall... the higher you bounce!"	Success is not easy, need to dream and learn from failures
24	Earl Nightingale—"Success is the progressive realization of a worthy ideal."	Continuous work toward goals

#	Definition	Key Words
25	Michael Dell—"You don't have to be a genius or a visionary or even a college graduate to be successful. You just need a framework and a dream."	Framework, dream, not genius
26	Ann Sweeney—"Define success on your own terms, achieve it by your own rules, and build a life you're proud to live."	A life you're proud of
27	Robert Collier—"Success is the sum of small efforts, repeated day in and day out."	Sum of repeated small efforts
28	Michelle Obama—"Success isn't about how much money you make. It's about the difference you make in people's lives."	Making a difference in lives of others
29	Woody Allen—"Eighty percent of success is showing up."	Showing up (action)
30	Malcolm Forbes—"Failure is success if we learn from it."	Learning from failure
31	Jon Bon Jovi—"Success is falling nine times and getting up 10."	Overcoming failures
32	Colin Powell—"Success is the result of perfection, hard work, learning from failure, loyalty, and persistence."	Hard work, learning from failure, loyalty, persistence
33	Benjamin Franklin—"Without continual growth and progress, such words as improvement, achievement, and success have no meaning."	Continuous improvement
34	Bill Bradley—"Ambition is the path to success. Persistence is the vehicle you arrive in."	Ambition, persistence

#	Definition	Key Words
35	Pele—"Success is no accident. It is hard work, perseverance, learning, studying, sacrifice and most of all, love of what you are doing or learning to do."	Hard work, perseverance, learning, sacrifice, love of what doing
36	Bobby Unser—"Success is where preparation and opportunity meet."	Preparation, opportunity
37	Henry Ford—"Coming together is a beginning; keeping together is progress; working together is success."	Working together
38	Virat Kohli—"Self-belief and hard work will always earn you success."	Self-belief, hard work
39	Shiv Khera—"Your positive action combined with positive thinking results in success."	Positive action and thinking
40	Napoleon Hill—"Patience, persistence and perspiration make an unbeatable combination for success."	Patience, persistence, perspiration (hard work)
41	Swami Sivananda—"Put your heart, mind, and soul into even your smallest acts. This is the secret of success."	Heart, mind, soul
42	Oprah Winfrey—"…How to be used in the greater service to life. Ask this question, and the answer will be returned and rewarded to you with fulfillment, which is the major definition of success, to me."	Greater service, fulfillment
43	Warren Buffett—"I measure success by how many people love me."	Love

#	Definition	Key Words
44	Mark Cuban—"To me, the definition of success is waking up in the morning with a smile on your face, knowing it's going to be a great day. I was happy and felt like I was successful when I was poor, living six guys in a three-bedroom apartment, sleeping on the floor."	Knowing it's going to be a great day, happiness
45	Dennis Waitley—"Total success is the continuing involvement in the pursuit of a worthy idea, which is being realized for the benefit of others—rather than at their expense." –*The Seeds of Greatness*, 1984, p. 21.	Continuous "involvement," worthy goals, benefit of others

APPENDIX B

SUCCESS RULES, KEYS, ELEMENTS FOUND ONLINE

#	Short Title of Article	Additional Information	Key Words NOT in Definition
1	Success Equation = Goals + Habits	Goals, sense of direction Habits, give mental discipline for action(s)	Habits
2	4 D's Formula of Success – Direction + Dedication + Devotion + Discipline	Direction seems to be goals; dedication and devotion seem to be synonyms; is discipline habit(s)?	Discipline (commitment)
3	3 Rules for Success – 1. Time matters, 2. Keep moving, 3. Have faith in yourself	Time is a resource; keep moving seems same as continuous improvement (progress) and have faith in yourself seems same as self-confidence!	Self-confidence
4	8 Proven Habits for Ultimate Success	Visualize your goals and rewire your beliefs	*Visualize* goals; beliefs

#	Short Tile of Article	Additional Information	Key Words NOT in Definition
5	10 Essential Rules for Success in Life	I thought this article was "pretty awesome" before realizing most were just excellent re-statements of what was already in the definition	Live with integrity and choose light over dark in Philosophy side of pyramid
6	7 Rules That Will Position You for Greater Success	Collaborate with others in Sociology side of pyramid; accept responsibility and be kind in Philosophy side of pyramid	Never neglect, "have no complacency"
7	A definition of success that includes hard work, having a healthy body, strong mind, willpower, and a positive attitude	The definition should include hard work (or deliberate practice) and having a healthy body	Willpower: determination, drive, self-control, positive attitude
8	Ultimate Success Definition	"Conclusive in a series or process; last, final; the highest or most significant"	Conclusion of goal
9	5 Keys to Success	All covered in definition including "build high esteem," "focus with a positive attitude" and "persevere"	To persevere is to persist, endure and stick (stickability); maintain *healthy* mind, body, and spirit

#	Short Tile of Article	Additional Information	Key Words NOT in Definition
10	5 Rules for Success	Not sure what means by "success has no limits" and "learn to see criticism as a sign of success"	Be account-able for your thoughts and actions; use fear as motivation to take action
11	First Rule of Success	Have a vision! Is this the same as a mission or purpose?	Vision
12	10 Golden Rules of Success	*Act with love*; focus on outputs, not inputs; take risks	*Love*, focus
13	6 Steps to Success in Life	Never get comfortable	"Reflect on yourself" and "stay curious"
14	The Secret of Success	"Letting go of all the things holding you back"	Let go
15	Five Elements of Success	"Believe you can do it" and "take *massive* actions"	Napoleon Hill often wrote about the impor-tance of belief (applied faith). Some research suggests "micro-actions" are important
16	The Key to Success	Preparation	Preparation: Added to definition

#	Short Tile of Article	Additional Information	Key Words NOT in Definition
17	7 Cardinal Rules of Success	"make peace with your past so it won't mess with your present" and "what others think of you is none of your business," "don't compare your life to others and don't judge them"	Make peace with past; don't compare or judge others
18	2 Rules for Success	1. Never tell everything you know	Can't use in definition, but an important "rule"
19	Maya Angelou's 5 Rules for Success	Do right; be courageous; *love self*; laugh; be a blessing	Do right; be courageous; love self; laugh; be a blessing
20	5 Keys to Success	Determination; skill; passion; discipline; luck	Already used in definition
21	11 Unexpected Ways to Define a Successful Person	*Work hard*; have focus; be humble; have a positive attitude	Already used in definition, except "be humble"
22	Define Success	View success as a process	Already used in definition
23	10 Tips to Become More Successful in Life	Be committed; learn from the journey; have fun; think positively; change your perspective; be honest with self; count on yourself	Take away distractions
24	Create Own Definition of Success	All definitions are same, but goals different	Already used in definition

#	Short Tile of Article	Additional Information	Key Words NOT in Definition
25	7 Rules of Success	*Love*; your attitude matters; learn every day; listen to your soul	Love; attitude
26	Golden Rules of Life	Let things sit; don't dwell on the past; acknowledge suffering, but don't let it take over	Every morning, think of one thing you can do today to take care of yourself
27	6 Keys to Success	Read something positive every day; have mentors; journaling and scheduling	Journaling; know the "why" of your goals
28	3 Things to be Successful	*Visualization* (critical step to success); believe (self-confidence); action	Already used in definition
29	7 Causes of Success	Take risks; unwavering self-belief; don't care what others think; think outside the box; optimistic at heart; resilient—not afraid of failure;	A "can do" attitude
30	3 Ways to be Successful	Refuse to remain the same person you were yesterday	Strive to grow; know-how and awareness of what's happening
31	3 P's of Success	Passion, preparation, persistence	All three covered in definition

APPENDIX C

NUMBER OF COMPONENTS IN THE VARIOUS LIFE BALANCE MODELS/ THEORIES

This table shows the theory/model, year of discovery, and information about the various components:

Key:

*Family & Home could go under "Social" with Social & Cultural

**Family and Community Support could go under "Social"

+Emotional would fit better under "Social"

++Contributions to Others could go under "Social" with Relationships

^Family could go under "Social" with Emotional

#Attitude could go under "Mind"

##Community/Charity could go under "Spiritual"

Researcher	Year	#	Body	Mind	Social	Soul	Other(s)
Alice Lloyd	1919	4	Physical	Mental	Social	Spiritual	
Danforth	1931	4	Physical	Mental	Social	Religious	
Maslow	1943	5	Physiological	Esteem	Belongingness & Love	Self-Actualization	Safety
Meyer	1960s	6	Physical & Health	Mental & Educational	Social & Cultural*	Spiritual & Ethical	Financial & Career Family & Home*
Caudill	1976	4	Physiology	Psychology	Sociology	Philosophy	
Waitley	1983	8	Physical	Mental	Social**	Spiritual	Financial Professional Family** Community Support**
Covey	1989	4	Physical	Mental	Social/ Emotional	Spiritual	
Pelletier	1997	10	Physical Fitness	Educational	Family	Spiritual	Attitude# Goals Leisure Financial Professional Community/ Charity##

Researcher	Year	#	Body	Mind	Social	Soul	Other(s)
Richardson	1998	6	Emotional+ & Physical Health	Fun & Adventure	Relation-ships	Spiritual Well-being	Work Contribu-tions to Others++
Kelly	1999	4	Physical	Intellectual	Emotional	Spiritual	
Kiyosaki	2001	4	Physical	Mental	Emotional	Spiritual	
McNeff	2021	7	Physical	Intellectual	Emotional	Spiritual	Family^ Professional Personal

APPENDIX D

HILL, MCCOY, ST. JOHN'S META-ANALYSIS

The following is a meta-analysis of Napoleon Hill's 17 Principles of Success, McCoy's 12 Megatraits of Successful People, and St. John's 8 Traits All Successful People Have in Common:

Key:

*Side of Caudill's pyramid in which traits best fit.

Bolded words were St. John's four secondary traits.

#	Napoleon Hill 1928	#	Doris Lee McCoy 1988	#	Richard St. John 2010	Side*
2	A Definite Chief Aim (Goal)	4	They're decisive, disciplined *goal setters*.	3, 10	Successful people have a *specific focus*. **Setting Goals****	Psychology
14	Profiting by Failure	3, 6	They use *negative experiences* to discover their strengths. They're persistent.	8	Successful people are *persistent* through failure.	All
7	Enthusiasm	1	They *enjoy* their work.	2	Successful people work hard while having fun.	All
3	Self-Confidence	2	They have a *positive attitude* and plenty of confidence.	9	**Positive Attitude**	Psychology
1, 13	The Mastermind Cooperation	9	They surround themselves with competent, responsible, and supportive people.	11	**Having Mentors**	Sociology
5, 16	Initiative & Leadership / Practicing the Golden Rule	5	They have integrity and help others succeed.			Sociology

#	Napoleon Hill 1928	#	Doris Lee McCoy 1988	#	Richard St. John 2010	#	Side*
11	Accurate Thinking						Psychology
12	Concentration	8	They've developed good communication skills and problem-solving skills.				All
6	Imagination			5	Successful people consistently come up with *new ideas.*		Psychology
9	The Habit of Doing More than Paid For			7	Successful people *provide value* to others.		Psychology
17	Cosmic Habit Force (Habits)			6	Successful people are constantly *getting better.*		All
		12	They have a sense of purpose and a desire to contribute to society.	1	Successful people are *passionate* about what they do.		All
4	The Habit of Saving	7	They take risks.		**Taking Risks**	**12**	Philosophy
8	Self-Control						All

#	Napoleon Hill 1928	#	Doris Lee McCoy 1988	#	Richard St. John 2010	Side*
10	A Pleasing Personality					Psychology
15	Tolerance					Sociology
		10	They're healthy, have high energy levels, and schedule time to renew themselves.			Physiology
		11	They believe in a higher power, or sometimes, just plain luck.			Philosophy

ABOUT
DONALD W. CAUDILL

Donald W. Caudill, Ph.D. Virginia Tech is a teacher, entrepreneur, author, speaker, consultant, coach, and philanthropist. He is currently a Professor of Marketing at Gardner-Webb University in Boiling Springs, North Carolina.

He can be reached at the book's email address:
thesuccesspyramid@yahoo.com

THANK YOU FOR READING THIS BOOK!

If you found any of the information helpful, please take a few minutes and leave a review on the bookselling platform of your choice.

BONUS GIFT!

Don't forget to sign up to try our newsletter and grab your free personal development ebook here:

soundwisdom.com/classics